Marriageology

Marriageology

THE ART AND SCIENCE OF
STAYING TOGETHER

———

BELINDA LUSCOMBE

SPIEGEL & GRAU
NEW YORK

Published in the United States by Spiegel & Grau,
an imprint of Random House, a division of
Penguin Random House LLC, New York.

SPIEGEL & GRAU and colophon is a registered
trademark of Penguin Random House LLC.

The appendix, from "The Experimental Generation of Interpersonal
Closeness" by Arthur Aron, Edward Melinat, Elaine N. Aron, Robert
Darrin Vallone, and Renee J. Bator from *Personality and Social
Psychology Bulletin* (1997) 23, 363–377, is reprinted by permission.

LIBRARY OF CONGRESS CATALOGING-IN-PUBLICATION DATA
Names: Luscombe, Belinda, author.
Title: Marriageology : the art and science of
staying together / by Belinda Luscombe.
Description: First edition. | New York : Spiegel & Grau, [2019] |
Includes bibliographical references.
Identifiers: LCCN 2018029424 | ISBN 9780399592362 |
ISBN 9780399592379 (ebook)
Subjects: LCSH: Marriage—Psychological aspects. | Couples—
Psychology. | Interpersonal relations. | Man-woman relationships.
Classification: LCC HQ734 .L87 2019 | DDC 306.81—dc23
LC record available at https://lccn.loc.gov/2018029424

Printed in the United States of America on acid-free paper

spiegelandgrau.com
randomhousebooks.com

2 4 6 8 9 7 5 3 1

FIRST EDITION

Book design by Dana Leigh Blanchette

TO EDO, WHO, THANK GOD,

PREFERS ENDURANCE SPORTS

Heart, are you great enough
For a love that never tires?

—ALFRED, LORD TENNYSON

Marriage is a wonderful institution, but
who wants to live in an institution?

—AUTHOR UNKNOWN,
BUT NOT TENNYSON

CONTENTS

Have you ever noticed how we celebrate marriage backwards? Wedding: big blowout party before heading off to lavish vacation. First anniversary, special and exciting, you might even get a note from relatives and friends. Second anniversary, dinner and a gift. And so it goes, with a traditional designated gift category (third: leather, fifth: wood, tenth: tin) until you get to fifteen years, for which the traditional gift is crystal. After fifteen, tradition no longer dictates an annual present. You're on your own, giftless, all the way to twenty, when you get china, which is less expensive than crystal. Then at thirty, the category is pearl, which basically means only the wife is receiving a gift.

This is all turned around. Any fool can be married for a year. You can get to three years on the fumes of the honeymoon alone. The time you really start to need wedding gifts is fifteen years in, when the novelty of having someone around all the time has worn off. Cutting off the presents at fifteen is like cheering people on for only the first half of a soccer game or until mile ten of a marathon. Those are the easy parts.

I was reminded of this backwardness when an old friend called. We hadn't spoken for a few months and he wanted me to know that he and his wife of twenty years were separating. They wanted to make it a really positive experience, he said, so they were going to live in the same house. They were still going to cook food for each other and do things together. Eventually they would separate their finances. They still loved each other, he insisted, they just couldn't be married. He pointed out that a mutual acquaintance was doing more or less the same thing.

This is now how marriages die: not in some fiery car crash of hatred, epic shouting matches, and slammed doors, with bloodied survivors staggering out of the smoking wreck into the arms of an EMT. Modern marital splits feel more like euthanasia in a high-end veterinarian's office. After a prolonged discussion about quality of life, the decision to end the union is made gently and with all the goodwill in the world, to put it out of its misery, much as an aged family pet is put down after his kidney function becomes unreliable and he keeps ruining the carpet. It's not done to rage against the dying of the marital light; conscious uncoupling is the thing.

My friend grieved, sure, but mostly he was embarrassed; it wasn't his first marriage. He has a grown son with his prior wife and he worried about what that son would think of him. As he talked about it, I got the impression that it felt to him more like losing a job than a family member. Or being careless with his credit card and getting scammed. *Again? Geez, what's wrong with me?*

Nobody likes to put it like this, but it is natural for marriages to fail. They can feel like the emotional equivalent of shoveling snow; people start strong and committed, but it takes so much more out of them than they expect. It is natural for people to get fed up with their marriages. It is natural for food to spoil, for a fire to go out, for enthusiasm to wilt.

After all, there is no bigger, no riskier, no more intimate decision a human makes than to say this is the person with whom I'm going to spend the bulk of my breathing time. This is the person with whom I'm going to create more humans. This is the person whose welfare I will now take into consideration in almost any decision I make. This is the person whose fortunes will affect mine, whose jokes and stories I will have to hear as long as I still have hearing, whose shoes will always be in my bedroom closet, whose hair will forever clog my drain.

In the era of the start-up, of the pop-up and the flash mob, a relationship that's supposed to last a lifetime can seem like an anomaly. It's too permanent. It doesn't lend itself to disruption. It does not allow you #failfast or upgrade. You'd think we'd have discarded it with all the other no-longer-useful human inventions like the walking plow and the fax machine and waiting a week for the next episode to arrive on TV.

But while it's natural for marriages to disintegrate, it is not inevitable. Nor is it desirable. We know how to keep food until we need it, or to tend a fire, or to motivate people. With some careful attention, nature can be surmounted.

And marriage, that fusty old institution, is worth fighting for. There is within most of us a deep desire to be in an intimate relationship with another person. Not to just have a playmate, but the full megillah, a husband or a wife or another warm body who is only ours and who cares for us as for no other, and who has promised to accompany us for the whole journey, all the way to the end of the map. Surveys show that getting married is still overwhelmingly the dream of young people (men and women alike). Lovers who move in with each other and like it usually still make it official, even though they don't need to. Marriage is so central to our conception of happiness that huge legal battles are being waged to this day to figure out whether people of the same sex may participate in it.

That's because, like a lot of things that go against nature—driving, scuba diving, pink hair—a marriage that lasts can be amazing. Life-changing, enriching, thrilling. Completely worth it.

But nobody scuba dives without help or instructions. Marriage, which has been historically so much more likely to fail than an oxygen tank, is the same.

I've been writing about and researching marriage for more than a decade for *Time* magazine. I've always found the subject fascinating because nearly everybody has a story about the institution that is central to their lives—whether it's their own marriage or their parents' or their children's or their best friend's or even their lover's. Marriage—by which I mean any exclusive lifetime commitment to one other soul, whether made official by the state or church or just between yourselves—pushes people to the extremes: humans can become their best selves, capable of great empathy and sacrifice. Or they can transform from nice regular neighbors into people capable of spectacularly petty and vengeful behavior.

Even as I have chronicled it, marriage has changed from an institution everybody expected to enter one day and muddle through, into a high-wire act—public, rewarding, quite difficult to pull off, and not actually all that necessary. Being single is easier and more acceptable than ever. There is no imperative to marry. What was a rite of passage has become a lifestyle choice—less trip to the supermarket, more excursion through a high-end artisanal farmers' market.

Marriage has been transformed by pressures from all sides: financial (the gig economy, the rising level of debt, the vagaries of the housing market, wage stagnation), technological (advances in medicine, particularly in fertility, online dating, social media), and sociological (the rising economic independence of women, the diminishing stigma associated with being unmarried or a single parent). Then there are the shock waves of globalism, massive digital innovation, and the information revolution; seismic shifts that have all shaped the intimate little bond between two people. Alongside those, a swarm of smaller changes have also buffeted its boundaries: the renaissance of the city, marriage equality, gender fluidity, Netflix, texting, the iPhone, Blue Apron, free online porn, #MeToo.

And yet amid all this turbulence, there are lots of reasons why getting married, or sticking for life with one person, is still a solid choice. Marriage is possibly the only institution that has been written about almost as widely in the academy as it has in books with pink spines. And studies find that it's really good for people, especially in the Three B's: body, bank, and bed. People who are happily paired with another live longer and are healthier, richer, and more satisfied with their life, in the main, than people whose relationships don't last. Their kids are more likely to thrive. They have (on average) more sex.

As with all great deals, however, there's some fine print: to get the benefits, you have to stay together, which is no simple matter. And you can't hate it—or each other. A Harvard study that has followed hundreds of Massachusetts men for eighty years (so far) found that the single best predictor of men's health at eighty was their satisfaction with their relationships at fifty. But it also found that living in a high-conflict marriage was akin to living in a war zone. People who are unhappily coupled are more miserable and less healthy than people who opted to stay single. The collapse of a marriage is recalled by those who endure it as the darkest passage of their lives.

Given all this, you'd think we would prepare for this exercise as seriously as we prepare for, say, a physics final. After all, you can remodel a house or move. You can change careers. Your hair will grow out. With a little effort you can put most unfortunate decisions behind you. But, especially if you have kids, there are very few ways to put a former life partner completely out of view, and almost certainly no legal ones.

Yet we somehow expect these relationships to just work out. People attempt to pick open the seams of their lives and their hearts and stitch this other person into them, and assume that the resulting garment will always be perfectly comfortable. They may not even notice that it has begun to fray until one day the whole thing just falls off, leaving them vulnerable and exposed.

The good news is that we have a lot of research into what makes a marriage work. Because of the centrality of that relationship in people's lives and the effect on children's welfare for many years afterward, sociologists, psychologists, relationship scientists, and those who study human behavior have examined the institution at length. While the desire to find a mate for life has not changed, the way that people go about it has; therefore, the research is always being updated and revised.

Many therapists have also written excellent books on the marriages they have observed and helped and how they have gotten couples out of quagmires. Instead of looking at a broad swath of behavior and drawing conclusions, these clinicians draw from a deep and intimate examination of what happens between two people. Are there problems that recur in many couples? Are there universal solutions? Usually their specialty informs what they observe: urban therapists may offer one perspective, faith-based counselors may come from a slightly different one, and sex therapists another. But their advice has commonalities and it often intersects with that of researchers'. If sociologists study the institution of marriage as if it were a mountain, therapists study it as if it were a thousand molehills. This book examines both perspectives and draws out the prevailing themes.

Over the years, I've tried to get to know marriage like a

foreign correspondent gets to know a country, making note of the patterns and the overlaps, figuring out what is universal to the human condition and what is particular to each couple. I've read countless studies and peer-reviewed journal articles and interviewed the researchers. I've spoken to therapists of all types, couples counselors, sex therapists, financial advisers. I've pored over statistics on marriage and argued with demographers about what they mean. I've tried to get to the bottom of what the divorce rate really is (for first marriages, probably somewhere north of 37 percent). I've talked to sociology professors, psychology professors, family studies professors, and at least one professor of consumer behavior. I've persuaded some statisticians to run their numbers for me a bit differently to bore into their data. I've also probed hundreds of the citizens of together-land about what it's like to live there, interrogating them about their money and their sex lives and their fights and their divorces and the way they worked out parenting. Boy, did people love wandering up to me at parties.

And of course, you can't really know a place until you've lived there. So I'm also drawing on my own marriage of a quarter century to a man who is very different from me. I know everybody says that, but here's how different: he and I went on one outing a year for seven years, each more excruciating than the last, before he finally said he couldn't understand why I didn't want to be his girl-friend. And I said something like: "Wait, *you like me?*" The last three decades or so have been an exercise in stringing a rope bridge over that communication chasm. There are still many treacherous gaps, but we usually make it across.

If you're standing in the bookstore reading this or looking at the preview online and you just want the answer in the next forty-five seconds as to whether or not you should leave your partner, then I have this for you: probably not. At least, not quite yet. The idea that a long relationship is worth something on its own has got a little tarnished recently. Partly that's because permanence is temporarily out of favor. We're all about disruption. Things that have been around for a while are no longer accorded honor simply because they've endured. But there are exceptions: beautiful cathedrals, old growth forests, vintage clothes. There are things that are worth fixing, or even better, maintaining. Your partnership may be one of them.

Someone should really come up with traditions for those in-between anniversaries. The gift industry has tried, but their ideas are garbage. The Chicago Public Library compiled a list that suggested a musical instrument for the twenty-fourth wedding anniversary. Thank you, Chicago, because nothing sets your heart afire like someone in your close proximity learning a new musical instrument. If we were being realistic about the latter years of marriage, we would choose items made of resin, which is toxic stuff that sets and becomes durable; or pumice, which is what extremely hot activity turns into; or quilts, which are all patches sewn together. Those are gifts that might mean something.

Until this terrible oversight is fixed, however, I have summarized what I've learned about being married into six subjects, six challenges all married or committed for life couples have to master, or at least grapple with, on their way to happily, or at least doably, ever after. Totally coincidentally, they're all F-words: familiarity, fighting, finances, family, fooling around (not my original title), and finding help. I can't guarantee they will fix everything or be simple to overcome. But I can guarantee they'll be more fun than learning the saxophone.

Marriageology

CHAPTER 1

———

Familiarity

My husband, Jeremy, does this thing with envelopes. He always asks if we have any, even
though I've shown him where they are a hun-
dred times. They're on the shelf, with the other stationery
items, near the pens, just above the photographs of our
children that we have duplicates of but still can't throw
out and menus that we also haven't thrown out. They've
been kept there for decades, in skinny ledges that resemble
mail slots. A complete stranger to our home, casting
around the room, would immediately detect that this was
the ideal envelope-holding situation. Doesn't matter.
Every time my spouse needs to mail something, he says,
"Do we have any envelopes?"

On the surface, it seems such an innocent question,
and the answer so easy. "Yes, sweetheart. They're on the

shelf, near the pens." But it makes me want to put stones in my pocket and walk into the ocean. Or even better, take them out and throw them at him.

Everything about his inquiry enrages and depresses me. Why can't he learn where they are? Why is his attention so much more precious than mine that I have to answer this every time? His whole passive-aggressive approach: "Do we have any envelopes?" is even more infuriating. He's not asking "Could you get me an envelope?" That would mean facing up to the fact that he has never bothered to learn a basic housekeeping fact. That would mean acknowledging that he is treating his spouse like his personal assistant. That would mean clearly spelling out that what he really wants *is for me to get him an envelope.*

"Do we have any envelopes?" is what my spouse says. What I hear is "Whatever I'm doing right now is vital, even if it's just random postage tasks. You, on the other hand, can't possibly be doing anything worthwhile. Bringing me the office supplies that are in the shelves behind me as I speak if I would just turn around and look is the kind of trivial scutwork right in line with your abilities."

How did this happen? I love this man. I have loved this man for years. I've never met anyone like him. He makes beautiful things, whether they are buildings or meals or children or adventures. He's handsome and strong and great in bed. He's patient and stoic. He makes up hilariously implausible theories about phenomena with very normal explanations and persists in pushing them in the face of overwhelming evidence. We have had two and a half decades of mostly happy coexistence. I'd be lost without him. So why does a small imperfection such as this set me off?

Because of familiarity. Familiarity is what you have when all the new relationship excitement has burned away like the boosters on a rocket and you've moved into an orbit in which your spouse rarely surprises you. It's what comes after the deep late-night talks about your hopes and desires have been replaced by negotiations on who is picking up the kids today. It's when a relationship is more commute than adventure, more meal planning than dining out. Familiarity is the natural byproduct of every marriage and in many ways a wonderful thing, like broken-in shoes. But it can be a huge drag and, if not handled well, can lead beyond boredom and frustration to far darker and more destructive territory. And for couples who want to be together for the long haul in our current era, familiarity is a bigger problem than it has ever been.

BREAKING NEWS: MARRIAGE IS CHANGING

The first time I heard anyone offer marital advice, I was terrified. I was a college student in the middle of a disastrous road trip. My friends and I had been trying to get to the mountains in my brother's ancient minibus, which usually made journeys no longer than up and down our driveway. The poor thing only lasted far enough out of town and late enough into the night that we could not call on anyone we knew for help, so while my friends waited with the vehicle, I ventured into the sole open establishment (this was before mobile phones), a local bar, full of workmen at the end of their shift, to find a phone and a tow truck. When I called, the driver told me to wait there.

As I waited, nursing my soda, a patron started talking loudly to nobody in particular, but, in the way of many prophets, to all of us. "Here's the thing about marriage," he told the room. "You always end up going back to your f***ing wife, because no other f***ing c**t gives a s**t about you." (For those guessing, yes, this was in Australia.)

It was a somewhat dark picture of our most celebrated romantic institution, but not completely out of character for the era. For prior generations, marriage was like my brother's bus; it was not the ideal vehicle for their dreams, but it was what they had. And for many couples—those more committed to maintenance, or those who chose their target destinations better than I did—it worked. My mother and father, married an impressive sixty years, never expected their union to be thrilling. I'd have been less shocked to hear my parents speaking elvish than saying "I love you" to each other. Even as a child I noticed the way my mother's voice flattened when she answered the phone—*Hello!*—and it turned out to be Dad: "Oh, it's you. What do you want?" I don't question their love or commitment, yet just before their fifty-ninth anniversary, I asked my mother the secret to a long marriage. "Tolerance," she said, without hesitating.

We no longer think about our lifelong unions this way. Gone are the days when you found a likely contender, tied the knot, and then weathered whatever storms or becalmed seas you encountered. Getting married is now seen as a promotion to a better type of life, like an upgrade to business class, with all manner of attendant perks. People want more from marriage than just a familiar face to come home to. They want fulfillment, stimulation, security, devotion, status, liberation, connection, collaboration, personal brand enhancement, transformation, and all the feels. "If the twentieth century marriage was *companionable,* the new marriage is *intimate,*" writes family therapist Terrence Real in his book *The New Rules of Marriage.* "Physically, sexually, intellectually, and above all, emotionally."[1] As the traditional marriage model— 1 breadwinner + 1 homemaker = 1 family—fades away, feeling has become more important. "The old model of marriage was that you got married for financial security and you tolerated each other. It was all about economic survival," psychotherapist Sue Johnson told me. "Now it's about emotional survival. Emotionless familiarity is not what people want."

But familiarity—emotionless or not—is part of the deal. It's both the reward of a long relationship and its burden. It can make us treat the person we are supposed to love carelessly. It can make us feel like our spouses are holding us back. It can blend into contempt. And in our modern era, which eschews the mundane and habitual for the novel and disruptive, the familiarity that's an inevitable part of life with another can feel more oppressive than welcome.

Northwestern University's Eli Finkel has studied modern marriage for years and concluded that what people want from their marriages in the twenty-first century lies beyond mere tolerance. It's enhancement. People want relationships that will make them more perfect versions of themselves. "We continue to view our marriage as a central locus of love and passion and we continue to view our home as a haven in a heartless world, but, for more and more of us, a marriage that achieves those things without promoting self-expression is insufficient," Finkel writes.[2] We don't want a person who knows us and accepts us as we are. We want a partner who knows us well enough to coach us into a better, more authentic version of who we are. A merely okay marriage is not enough. Just like to-

day's coffee and today's bread, today's marriages are expected to be of a higher quality.

Why do people keep demanding more from their marriages? One theory[3] suggests it has to do with relational
mobility. In societies in which people can easily change
partners, such as the United States, partners seek and express more passion because they want to shore up the relationship; it's a way of keeping their partners interested
and warding off others. In Japan, on the other hand, there
are generally lower emotional expectations from marriage
because it's more difficult to switch partners. (Japanese
law does not allow for joint custody.)

A more demanding and exciting relationship is fine, of
course, except that it's pretty much impossible for one
person to continually provide to another 100 percent
guaranteed emotional satisfaction, especially for as long
as you both shall live, especially with how long many of us
are living. We all want more from a spouse than one
human could possibly dispense. And when we don't get it,
we're shocked. "It's become more difficult for our marriage to live up to our expectations, which means that
more of us end up feeling disappointed," notes Finkel.[4]
These unreasonable presumptions are not entirely our
fault. All of us have for years been sold this phony bill of
goods, catfished into believing in the existence of the soulmate.

LET'S KILL ALL SOULMATES

Here is my idea for a good way to drive people mad: get them to believe there is only one right car for them. Not one make or model, but one actual car. And they have to find it. When located, it would make them giddily happy whenever they drive. If, on the other hand, they didn't find the car, or if somebody else owned it and didn't want to sell it, or they inadvertently settled for an automobile that was not quite perfect, then the drivers might have wheels to get around in, but they would always in some sense be stuck with a lemon.

How would you get people to believe such a crazy thing? Easy: just craft a lot of beautiful stories about people finding their One True Auto. Have people sing about driving it home, at last. Get car buyers to believe that it will come fully loaded and never need a mechanic or run out of gas or break down. It would help if you could create a network of potential cars that these seekers could access and browse so that their search could go global and their specifications could be exactly met. People could enter their preferences—four-wheel drive, fuel efficiency, suicide doors, a blue light around the base—and suggestions would be delivered right to their personal computing device.

Then, set up a tradition where people would have an enormous party when they signed the contract and all their friends would come and throw things at them and take photos and the new car owner would wear an insanely expensive outfit they'd never use again.

And of course, if the automobile ever failed to make the driver happy, if it got a scratch or the seatbelt got stuck or that stupid brake light kept flickering, the car owner could off-load it but would lose a lot of money on it.

Obviously, that's bonkers. People would either never buy a car or just trade in endlessly, making themselves crazy. Believing that there's just the one car or pair of pants or haircut or bottle of beer that is perfect for you is a great way of never wearing pants or drinking beer again.

In the same way, the search for a soulmate is fruitless and destructive. A soulmate is not a thing. At least, it's not a thing you can find. That's a myth trafficked to us by folks who need to peddle movie tickets and iTunes downloads and subscriptions to eHarmony. The chances that you have somehow located, attracted, bonded with, and contractually bound yourself to the *only* person who is the one perfect match for you are vanishingly small.

We don't find soulmates, like some fantastic shell on the beach. We become them. And as we do, the other person becomes ours. One of us is the waves and the other is the sand, and together we make the beach, changing the shape and passage of the other and maybe even bringing some amazing conches to the surface alongside the seaweed and knotted fishing wire.

This does not mean, however, that your partner is going to make you whole. He or she is not going to catapult you into a different version of you, one in which you are always happy, or always on time, or never make mistakes. You may think you've found the perfect combination of sexpot/chef/nurturer and now all your problems are solved, but it is not so. That's not what you're doing when you're getting married. Marriage means you've thrown your lot in with a person and said, "This journey looks like it might be more fun with you."

Carol Dweck, a psychologist at Stanford University, has a theory about fixed and growth mindsets. A fixed mindset is one in which people believe their abilities and interests and intelligence are set from birth. A growth mindset is one in which people believe that interests and abilities can be cultivated. Those with a fixed mindset spend a long time looking for their passion or their career. Those with a growth mindset tend to work at things longer and build on them. Marriage requires a growth mindset. You have not set up your life with *the* one, you have set it up with *some*one. From here, you work on perfecting communication and adoration and appreciation of eccentricities.

As a rule of thumb, it's helpful to realize that nearly everything about your partner will, at some point, enrage you beyond reason. They won't change when you want them to. They'll change when you don't want them to. The more that you get to know them, the more the things that charmed you in the first place will become the things that make you want to set your own hair on fire just to get away from them for five minutes. You don't solve the problem of familiarity by choosing the right person—although for the love of mercy, please select carefully—you solve it by choosing what you will do when the blinkers come off and you realize that this is the person who is going to be in your life for the rest of your life.

When I first met my husband, I loved how much he adored what he did. It was intoxicating, all that passion for architecture. My dad, who was in reinsurance, which he called the "not terribly exciting end" of insurance, was a solid provider but had less than no inclination to discuss his work. Every night he would quiz my mother, a teacher, for the details of her day instead. My husband, on the other hand, was animated by what he did. It thrilled him. He was really good at it and jazzed by how good other people were at it. His enthusiasm was infectious, and I would join him on his trips to out-of-the-way art bookstores (remember those?), little-known buildings, and even—such was my crush—lectures.

Eventually, however, I wearied of the way all conversational and leisure and life-planning roads led to architecture. I yearned for some small talk about music or the weather, or a nice desert vacation or deep-sea trip, anywhere with no buildings. But you can't have the invigorating parts of a deep passion without the oh-for-Pete's-sake-this-again parts. They are two sides of the same quoin.

And of course, I am no picnic. I am that person who handles almost every situation by trying to see the humor in it. People like that. It can liven up a gathering or lighten a dark moment. It's handy for writing on deadline. And, in fact, the right kind of humor can be an asset for making marriages last.[5] But then again, sometimes the person who sees the humor in everything is just insensitive. She's not who you want in that serious meeting, or in intimate discussion about something awkward and painful, or telling a story about you to associates. It can be very damaging to the durability of marriages.[6] It can be a huge drag.

I'd say I miss the comedy sweet spot about 70 percent of the time and do serious damage to a person's feelings at least 12.5 percent. Those percentages are better than in my youth, but I just can't figure out which are the one-in-eight times I should definitely shut up. And even if I could, constitutionally, never go for the joke around the people I love, it would feel like a dereliction of care. What kind of monster never tries to make her family laugh?

It's not just that we cannot change our spouses; it's that really, we wouldn't want to. The things we love about them are organically bonded to the things that make us bananas. Is your spouse incredibly fit? Then you'll be driven batty by how much time he or she spends exercising. Is your spouse gorgeous? You'll find the attention from strangers galling. Love your partner's creativity? Oy, the mess. Is your spouse really organized and tidy? Man, the fussing!

FAMILIARITY'S NASTY FRIEND

Most people accept that boredom, frustration, and disappointment are inevitable by-products of familiarity, just as my mother did. They're problematic but manageable. They might grind you down but will likely not make you split up. The real problem with familiarity is that it is the breeding ground of contempt. You've probably seen contempt in some of the couples around you. You know, when you go to that dinner party or brunch or kid's soccer match, and suddenly the playful spousal banter gets sharp and one person is staring intently at his or her lap, trying not to lose it. Contempt is one of the biggest marriage-slayers, inflicting wounds and sapping the joy out of the partners toward whom it is expressed. One woman told me she decided never to get married again after she heard contempt in her husband's voice just one time, because of how corrosive it felt.

Contempt is a weaponized version of taking someone for granted. Respect sounds so formal and impersonal and yet it gets at a basic human desire: to be known *and* loved at the same time. To be somebody's beloved even when he or she has seen you with crusty eyes or scratching your genitals or after a nasty three-day flu. It's one thing to disdain a sports or political figure you don't care for. It's another to denigrate or belittle somebody you have lived, eaten, slept, and mated with. And marriage is a ruthlessly efficient tool for aiding people to inflict scorn. Very few institutions allow members to gather so much opposition research about each other and simultaneously give them so many opportunities to use it. Very few humans can drop contempt bombs on each other with as deadly aim as those who have been married. Siblings come close, but they don't live in such close quarters for as long.

A friend told me she knew she had to leave her husband when she began to bristle at the way he ate pasta. He crunched it somehow; she could hear it from clear across the room. It set her on edge. She's not alone; the psychiatrist Phil Stutz has said that the beginning of the end of the relationship is when one partner is disgusted by the other partner's mouth. There's a neurological condition known as misophonia, in which otherwise neutral or trivial sounds trigger anxiety and stress in people. Neuroscientists believe that when sufferers hear their trigger sounds, the part of the brain that controls subjective emotions—disgust, fear, sadness—is also activated. My friend's ex-husband wasn't eating pasta loudly; the noise of it was triggering the disgust she was already feeling toward him.

The Chewing Noise Divorce made more sense to me when I came across a small but nifty 1980s experiment[7] in which some trained observers were placed in couples' homes to observe and make note of only positive exchanges. The couples they were watching were also trained to record their own positive interactions. Happy couples came up with data that closely matched the researchers' about how many good moments they'd had. Those who were unhappy recorded only half as many. Fully 50 percent of the communications that the researchers had regarded as positive, the unhappy couples saw as negative.

A psychologist at the University of Oregon, Robert Weiss, called this "negative sentiment override."[8] It's where our negative feelings override our cognitive abilities and we interpret our spouses' statements or behavior (or maybe eating noises) in the darkest possible way, even if they are neutral or positive. It's the opposite of seeing things through rose-colored glasses; instead we can only recognize that which we hate.

Over hundreds of thousands of interactions with the

same human being, we develop a narrative for how they function. This is normal and natural; it saves us cognitive energy when we have that exchange again. I know that my spouse cannot multitask—he will not converse while he's cooking or texting—and that if he's shouting obscenities from another room, it's good news, because home maintenance is under way.

But these internalized narratives can also be dead wrong, especially if what our spouse does upsets or grates on us. What we assume he or she is saying or doing is often not at all what he or she intended. I have friends who had this problem with bread. She complained that her husband gave her the outside piece of the loaf, the crust, the part that nobody wanted. But it turned out that in his family, that was considered the best part. What he assumed was an act of generosity, she took as a sign that she wasn't worth soft bread. Why on earth would her husband want her to have the worst piece of bread? There is no reason. It's just negative sentiment override.

How do you get out of that negative cycle and banish contempt when there are no mysteries between you, no thrilling new little things you didn't know you had in common, no respite from being nibbled to death by a person's dozens of irreparable grating flaws?

YOU'RE ALLOWED TO CHANGE YOUR MIND

One crucial conscious choice would be to decline to ascribe a bad intention to your spouse's actions. Except in extremely rare circumstances, your spouse is not out to get you. Nor, probably, to deliberately irritate you. I know it's sometimes hard to believe this. No rational person could believe my spouse can't remember where envelopes are kept, for example. But I have come to find his enquiries amusing. The man simply lives in a stationery-free world. It is his blind spot, his "mail gaze," so to speak. His inability to recall the whereabouts of paper goods is not actually a reflection of what he thinks of me. It's a reflection of what he thinks of envelopes. And now I almost think of it with fondness, this postal incompetence. It's like the birthmark on his chin, a harmless idiosyncratic blemish. (I suppose it doesn't hurt that we rarely need to send letters anymore.)

Another tip that therapists and studies both support is for couples to use familiarity as a tool rather than a weapon. Couples who see themselves as a team, as partners engaged in a common enterprise, are often able to do this more easily. That is, you're not hanging out with a person just because it feels good or makes you happy. You're making something—a marriage or a family or a couple, or whatever iteration of a long-term committed partnership you're attempting.

In fact, Carl Whitaker, one of the godfathers of family counseling, used to compare the family unit to a sports team that's been playing together for a long time: they know each other's moves, so they're powerful in their connectedness. That's why there are some teams that are better than others. The '90s Chicago Bulls, the '70s West Indian cricket team, the 1997 Brazilian soccer team. It's not that those individual players are all better (although it doesn't hurt to have a Michael Jordan or a Ronaldo), it's that they worked together as a unit. They were better as the Bulls than just as Jordan, Pippen, and Jackson.

With a team mentality, it's much easier to do things that you often find tedious. That's where the phrase "taking one for the team" originates. Baseball players hit the sacrifice fly, ice hockey players draw a penalty, domestiques in a cycling team wear themselves out pulling their lead rider to the front of a race. They do this not just because they like the particular athlete whom they are advancing from second to third base or for whom they are getting that yellow Lycra jersey, but because they want the team to do well. The team is the point. In the same way, there is your lover and then there is the partnership you have made together, the marriage or the relationship, which has its own value. You're not just there for him or her or you, but also for some third thing that exists beyond the two of you.

This kind of "relationship thinking," as it's called, is key to a long and happy-ish union. It has even been shown to have a biological effect. A small study[9] of Texan women in 2009 found that when they thought about their relationship with their romantic partner they registered an increase in salivary cortisol, which researchers think is one of the body's responses to being passionately in love.

That's what a relationship can be: more than the sum of its two humans. And when people think of it like that, it's easier to respect their person, to want to work with them and to not find them grating. It's easier to do the tiny corny things that actually make a difference.

TINY CORNY THINGS THAT ACTUALLY
MAKE A DIFFERENCE

With any habitual behavior, the easiest way to change it is to start small. Making a few slight tweaks to the way you treat your spouse can have a huge payoff. For example, here's a technique that every person who wants to make their relationship last should master. It takes a little getting used to, but most people can eventually manage it with practice: 1. Notice something good your spouse did. (Actively look for it, if you have to.) 2. Thank them for doing it. 3. Do not immediately follow this expression of gratitude with any caveats, if at all possible. ("Thanks so much for cooking dinner but I think you used up all the good Parmesan": UNACCEPTABLE. "Thanks so much for lighting the fire": ACCEPTABLE.)

It sounds implausible and greeting card–esque, but there is solid research that suggests simply saying thank you to your spouse makes a big difference. A 2015 study[10] from the University of Georgia Center for Family Research found that expressing gratitude toward your spouse was "the most consistent significant predictor of . . . marital quality." Researchers called about five hundred American couples and asked them about stresses in their relationship and how they handled them. And they found that saying thank you had a sort of protective effect, despite the fact that the couple may have financial stress or were fighting. "Even if a couple is experiencing distress and difficulty in other areas," said lead author Allen Barton, "gratitude in the relationship can help promote positive marital outcomes." It makes sense, too. If you say thank you to someone, you can't also be taking him or her for granted. Or at least, they will feel like you're not.

Another study,[11] from Florida State University in 2011, found that thanking a partner led to a more positive perception of that partner. Participants who were assigned to express more gratitude to their partners felt better about that person than participants who were not asked to be grateful. That positive perception also led to the thanker's feeling more comfortable about raising things that needed work in the relationship. This, in turn, lowered resentment in the thanker. Resentment acts on human connection like a wet sock acts on a foot. It causes friction. Gratitude is like moleskin, the soft padding you put around blisters to make sure you can keep hiking or running or just plodding along. It's a resentment buffer.

Eventually, just like your mom said, thanking your partner becomes a reflex, so that you're making your spouse feel good *without even realizing it,* which is like marital nirvana. Researchers at the Gottman Institute, probably the most widely recognized marital research and training organization in the United States, have put the optimal ratio of negative to positive interactions at 1:5. That is, for every time you say something snippy to your spouse, you have to say or do five nice things. I find early in the morning, right after you both get home from work, and last thing at night are really easy times to get three of those out of the way. Did you sleep well? I'm so glad you're (or I'm) home! And then your chosen version of good night. Doesn't hurt a bit. Two more of those and it's safe to talk about the unfolded laundry.

Another very simple practice: celebrate your spouse's victories. One big-shot marital researcher I interviewed proudly talked about the time his wife's paper got accepted in a highly prestigious academic journal and he printed out the email notification poster-size and stuck it on the front door. This works because you are not only appreciating your spouse, but you are absorbing and enacting your admiration for him or her. It has a positive effect on both of you. And it lines up nicely with Finkel's observations about the modern ideal of having a partner who brings out and enhances the better version of you.

Ironically, another way to "consciously couple," as some marital gurus with showbiz connections now call it, is to ask your spouse to do you a favor. This sounds counterintuitive, but it is an actual phenomenon with a name: the Franklin effect. It's said that Benjamin Franklin, aware that a member of the cabinet disliked him, asked to borrow a rare book that he knew the guy owned. After the book was returned, with a note, the lender was always warmer to Franklin.

There is research that suggests that getting people to do you a favor helps them to feel more positive about you. In a famous experiment[12] from the sixties, two researchers held a contest for prize money, then treated the winners three different ways. One group was asked personally by "the researcher" (or a guy playing the researcher) to return the prize money, since it was his own and he was a little hard up, another was asked by an "office secretary" (or a person playing one) to return the money because the department budget was tight, and a third wasn't contacted. After the three groups were surveyed, Group 1, those who had done him a personal favor, felt the warmest toward the researcher. Group 2, who had dealt with the secretary, felt the least warm and Group 3 was in the middle.

The reason the favor technique works, some researchers believe, might lie in self-perception theory. Helping someone out makes us feel like the person we want to be, the kind of person we believe we are. We are someone who is needed, on whom other people call for help. That's why it's key that it's couched as a favor, not an expectation. (And obviously does not require *too* much added labor.) It's also much more effective when the favor is not some onerous task anybody could do but one that acknowledges your spouse's strengths. "Honey, how would you solve this issue I'm having with a colleague?" would fall into this category. "Can you vacuum the car?" would not.

Scott Stanley, therapist, research professor, and codirector of the Center for Marital and Family Studies at the University of Denver, says one of his favorite techniques is to get one partner to carry out some small but unusual action for the other without even being asked. "I often tell people, 'Try to think of one thing you can do for them this week that they like and you don't normally do, that's actionable,'" he told me. It could be as small as making the bed, or taking the kids out so they can sleep in. This works, he believes, on two fronts: 1) because of the aforementioned Franklin effect and (2) it gets partners to think about what their spouse's day is like, what their current pressures might be, and to therefore have some empathy for them. Generosity and marriages go together, studies[13] have shown, more or less like water and a slip and slide; they make each other more fun.

Another perhaps less obvious practice that is supported by research is prayer. Not the "Please Lord, make it stop" kind, but prayer that focuses on the partner's well-being. One recent study[14] found that people who prayed for their spouses more often reported having a less stressful marriage than those who prayed for them less often. Another, from 2014, looked at more than two hundred African American couples who had been married for more than ten years, and found that couples who prayed for each other had more marital satisfaction and higher levels of commitment.[15] Still another showed that couples who took marriage education programs with prayer had more marital satisfaction than those who did the education without it.[16]

Brian Ogolsky, an associate professor in human development and family studies at the University of Illinois Urbana-Champaign, who surveyed fifty years' worth of studies on relationship maintenance, was surprised by how solid the data on prayer was. "The guys who are doing this work are pretty well-known in the relationship realm and are not at religious institutions," he told me. "If you had asked me what I thought about this five years ago, I would have said, 'Ah no.'" Scholars have suggested this technique might work because it's undertaken by people who are religious and therefore already committed to the idea of marriage, or because it gets people to think about their partner or a conflict with the partner in a different, more compassionate way. It's also possible the meditative effects of prayer are similar to those of mindfulness and breathing techniques. And of course, there's always a chance it's help from upstairs.

IT'S NOT JUST WHAT YOU DO TO YOUR SPOUSE, IT'S WHAT YOU DO WITH THEM

One model of relationship science, known as the self-expansion model, suggests that the thrill experienced during those early romantic days arises from the intense development of closeness. Arthur Aron, a psychology professor at State University of New York, Stony Brook, and one of the fathers of this school, explained it to me like this: "There are two things that are part of what we've evolved to do. One is to survive and the other is to develop new identities and understandings and abilities so we can be more effective, live longer, and live better. So one motivation we have in life is to expand the self, to increase our ability to accomplish things. One of the ways we do that is by forming relationships." The brain is galvanized by all the new information it's taking in about another human so fast that new lovers feel more alive to the sensations around them. Obviously, though, that learning curve flattens over time—and so does the excitement.

Aron and colleagues theorized that getting couples to do exciting things together, to learn new stuff, might enhance the relationship. The idea is that when you get your brain working on an activity that it finds arousing—or, as they would put it, expand the self in proximity to your partner—your brain draws pleasure from that and, in turn, associates that pleasure with your partner.

They tested[17] the theory on fifty-three middle-aged married couples who spent ninety minutes a week engaged in a proposed activity. Some couples chose from a list of "exciting" activities—skiing, hiking, dancing, or going to concerts. Another group did "pleasant" stuff such as going to the movies, eating out, or visiting friends. A third group did nothing different. The couples who participated in the exciting activities experienced higher levels of marital satisfaction during the study. So it worked, at least in the short term.

If you think this idea—find ways to associate your partner with good times—sounds unlikely, you're not alone. A psychology professor at Florida State University, James McNulty, was also dubious. McNulty and his team of researchers were asked by officials at the Department of Defense if they could come up with any ideas to help the marriages of military personnel who were deployed in stressful situations and separated from their spouses. (One study[18] has shown that the likelihood of divorce among combat veterans is 62 percent higher than among other veterans.) They decided to experiment[19] with changing the feelings people associated with their loved ones.

They asked some couples to look at photos of their partners alongside various other images, such as puppies, pizza, babies, and the word *wonderful* every three days for six weeks. Other couples saw a photo of their spouses alongside a neutral image, like a button. Every two weeks the researchers did a gut check on the participants to see what they associated their spouses with: happy thoughts or sad ones. Those who got the positive image connected their spouses with more positive things as the experiment went on. And they reported feeling better about their marriages.

Alas, McNulty doesn't feel that the effect is powerful enough for the research to be developed into a marriage-saving app, in which you look at photos of baby pandas and your spouse at the same time and live happily ever after. But it shows how important, and malleable, people's gut feelings about their spouses are.

The reverse seems to also apply. People who associate their spouses with drudgery have less happy marriages. In one longitudinal study[20] researchers looked at 123 married couples over a nine-year span and found that those who said their marriage was boring in the seventh year of marriage had less marital satisfaction by the sixteenth year. This was true for both men and women and across races and income. The reason, the researchers believed, was that the boredom had led to less closeness. Getting bored with your spouse means you spend less time with them, which then makes you less close.

Therapists tell me that even the planning of future activities draws people closer. That's kind of what commitment is, a vision of togetherness for the long haul. "Commitment is, in huge part, about believing in a future," says Scott Stanley. "Talking and thinking about your future together reinforces it." That shared horizon supports the relationship-enhancing notion discussed earlier in the chapter that you are playing on a team.

The suggestion that you try to learn new activities with your spouse is by no means novel. It borders on cliché. But it is more endangered than it ever was by the allure of solitary digital diversions. Getting out and doing stuff requires dedication and sometimes cash, while playing Candy Crush or posting on Instagram or watching Netflix does not. There are more rivals for our leisure time than ever and we carry them with us wherever we go. Social media, for example, is a double-edged sword. Scrolling through other people's feeds is a handy hedge against boredom and loneliness, but it can keep us from making an effort with those who are too conveniently close by to prioritize or make them seem dull in comparison.[21] It can widen our circle and offer support and perspective that our spouses sometimes can't provide, but it can also divert our attention from interacting or taking initiative with our lovers. And our partners' online personae can be a fascinating periscope into how they see the world or wish to be seen, but they can also be alienating and make us feel excluded.

Of course, those digital pursuits don't have to be solitary. Social media offers plenty of ways to connect with your spouse. Couples have created Instagram feeds together or follow similar interests. Facebook chief operating officer and Lean In founder Sheryl Sandberg says that when her husband died, one of the things she really missed was playing online Scrabble with him. Many couples play videogames together; the Internet is full of lists of the best ones for duo play. None of these, however, should transplant adventures that are actually new.

And those adventures don't have to just be for the two of you. Studies have found that couples who are close friends with other couples tend to have much happier marriages and survive a lot of rough terrain. "Having friendships with other couples is really beneficial to the relationship," Aron told me. This would fit his self-expansion theory, because you're learning about other people alongside your partner, but also generally makes sense; the members of the other couple can be a sounding board, they can be an avenue for venting, they can join the celebrations, they can create a frame of reference.

In 2015, Aron was briefly in the center of the media spotlight for a suite of thirty-six questions that he'd developed that he surmised would accelerate intimacy between couples because to answer them, people had to be prepared to be vulnerable. Mutual vulnerability is the most reliable shortcut to closeness. (This is also why people in the early throes of love often stay up all night telling each other their secrets.) The list included such queries as:

When did you last sing to yourself? To someone else?

If you were able to live to the age of ninety and retain either the mind or body of a thirty-year-old for the last sixty years of your life, which would you want?

Do you have a secret hunch about how you will die?

If you could wake up tomorrow having gained any one quality or ability, what would it be?

Name three things you and your partner appear to have in common.

What is your most treasured memory?

What is your most terrible memory?[22]

People began using these questions to get to know their college roommates, their in-laws, a whole slew of things. But it can be awkward to spring them on someone you already know quite well. (I tried them with my mother. It went badly.) So Aron has another suggestion: "It turns out that one of the things that can be really powerful is to do these questions as a foursome with another couple," he says. These are the types of things you might learn about someone eventually while just hanging out, but the learning curve is much steeper, which the brain likes. (*For a full version of the quiz, please see the appendix.*)

SAVE SOME OF YOU FOR YOU

This brings us to the question of whether you should heed that other old marital advice and try to take an interest in your spouse's hobbies. The scholarship on this says both yes and no. In a perfect world, a passion shared by the person with whom you're going to spend your life is a pastime devoutly to be wished. In reality, however, research[23] has found that a lot of the so-called "shared" passions end up being the husband's. The wife, in attempting to enhance the relationship, goes along with the husband's preferences and does not insist on her own. Why are wives more likely to compromise their interests? Because it feels easier. "Giving in is one common way women handle the collision of the twenty-first-century expectations with a twentieth-century mate," writes Terrence Real.[24] The problem arises when women who never get to choose what to do begin to feel resentment, a necessary and sufficient precondition of contempt.

Moreover, attempting to do everything with your spouse presents a high degree of difficulty and a danger zone for dreariness. Feel free, or even obliged, to have some interests of your own. I'm interested in architecture now, and can talk about the work of Frank Gehry and Zaha Hadid with a degree of erudition. I notice form, can see beauty in brutalism, and, given enough time to rotate the image, can *almost* make sense of an architectural plan. But I will never love it like my husband does. Somewhere around the discussion of the interplay of circulation with the programmatic elements, I get a little twitchy. He, on the other hand, pays more attention than before we met to current affairs, the stuff I watch and write about obsessively every day. I wouldn't call him a news junkie, but he's become a recreational user. He initiated me into backpacking. I initiated him into the joys of the beachside vacation.

But I do not have the patience for the esoteric cooking techniques he loves or any of the tennis grand slams; he has been to yoga exactly twice, once for my birthday, and knows nothing of our culture's iconic comedy. You could say to the man "Stop trying to make fetch happen" and he'd draw a complete blank. That's okay. Lord knows there are plenty of people to argue the relative merits of the oeuvres of Buck Henry and Amy Schumer. I don't need my spouse to love everything I love. But that does not mean I need to give them up either. Differences are what make you interesting to each other. Try—amid all the other things you have to do—to keep brewing your own particular cups of tea. Divorce lawyer James Sexton writes in his book *If You're in My Office, It's Too Late* that he has seen too many people whose unhappiness with their marriage stemmed from having mothballed the parts of themselves that brought them joy. Try to do different stuff from your spouse. As Sexton writes: "You can't end every night with, 'Oh, I forgot to tell you that crazy story about when we both sat next to each other and watched Netflix until just now.'"

Likewise, I can't fix, or even understand, all of my spouse's problems. He has complicated negotiations with clients and contractors and city officials that make my eyes water with the tedium. And he can't fix mine. He can't stop editors deleting my favorite phrases or make people call me back. Nor do I want him to. One of the biggest mistakes guys particularly make when their spouses come to them with an issue is to adopt a mend-it mentality. They're sick of hearing about it and they want the problem solved, so they can move on to something else. But a lot of problems aren't solvable, or not easily. Often partners just want someone to listen to them, to share the knowledge of the burden, because it feels then that they're not carrying it alone. There are so many times when all your life partner needs to hear is this: "That sounds hard." Or "Oh, babe." When I failed my first American driving test, despite having being a licensed driver in another country for a decade and a half, I texted my husband, mortified. "Aw. I kiss you," he said. That bought him so many envelope-fetchings.

This does not mean that spouses should spurn all of their lovers' attempts to fix things, however. Saying to your partner "I just want you to listen, not help" is depriving them of half the ways they can show love.

Sometimes conversation about your spouse's woes might be boring and maddening and exhausting. To which I say, lucky you, that you have someone who trusts you enough to share even the quotidian. Listen up. Responsiveness has been linked in numerous studies to deeper relationship satisfaction in all sorts of ways, including greater self-esteem[25] and greater sexual interest.[26] Think of it as going online to try to get tickets for a Beyoncé concert. There's a lot of refreshing the browser and waiting around and thinking that it costs too much, but then, you get to see Beyoncé live. We make these sacrifices all the time if we think it's worth it, and there's no way forming an intimate lifetime bond with another human is not going to be worth it.

This is what love is, actually. Not a fluttery feeling for someone or a lot of affection for how a person can give you affirmation—although those things are, God knows, very handy—but a willingness to throw down for that person, a conscious decision, dammit, to do whatever you can to make that person's life a little better, more fun, less stressful. John Gottman (after whom the institute is named) says the real marriage ninjas are the spouses who do not just respond to their spouses' requests—he calls them "bids"—for connection, but are constantly scanning the horizon for something that may affect their spouses, preempting their bid. We do this with our kids all the time. We try to figure out ahead of time what they might need or be going through. We also tolerate a lot of ho-hum for them. I don't want to go to the park, or play this endless pointless game about princesses, or push toy cars around, or watch *Frozen* again and I especially do not want to stand here and push you on this swing because it's both tiring *and* boring. But we do it, because there is such joy in loving someone and being able to make them happy. This is at the heart of so much of what makes a marriage work, of sex, of money, of raising kids, of fighting. Can we choose this person's desires over our own?

LIFE LESSONS FROM A LITTER BOX

I cannot tell you to stop being bored by your spouse, but I can tell you about the human propensity for hedonic adaptation—our inability to find things very wonderful (or very awful) for very long. Humans, it's believed, have a relatively stable level of happiness, which can be temporarily lowered by a setback (be it accident, job loss, or nasty facial blemish) or temporarily raised by a stroke of good fortune (lottery win, great parking spot, pants on sale), but will eventually return to more or less where it was beforehand. This might be easier to explain with the aid of our cat box. We have two rescue cats—Octopus and Platypus. We have spent a small fortune on them, and in gratitude they regularly put on a show of their two most astonishing skills: one is vomiting, and the other is timing their digestion so one of them always hits the litter box just as we sit down to eat. The black cat, Platypus, developed an allergy to all the proteins he had ever tried before, which is just preposterous and must be some kind of joke that all veterinarians are in on, so he can eat only rabbit. Of course, that means you have to feed both cats rabbit, since cats are notorious vomit sharers. Have you ever wondered what a rabbit uses as a defense mechanism to ward off would-be predators? Well, I think I've figured it out: they smell lethal after they've been digested. Any predator that had to clean up after him- or herself would never eat a bunny again.

The noxious odor, the digestive timing, and the positioning of the litter box, which for various boring reasons couldn't be moved from right near where we ate, conspired to make domestic life at our house intolerable. We talked about cat waste every day. We tried different litter. We tried rotating cleaning shifts. We consulted vet friends. Didn't matter; the cat box continued to wreak domestic havoc and dominate every conversation over every meal. I suggested to my husband that he treat the issue as a design challenge. He suggested euthanasia. When I countered that this seemed extreme, he clarified that he meant for the cats.

Eventually we spent way too much—I mean half a thousand dollars—on an enormous automatic self-cleaning contraption from Canada, the Litter-Robot III Open Air. If you think it sounds ridiculous, you are not wrong. It is the ugliest thing we own, if you don't count the cat vomit. But it works. Hardly any smell, no arguing over whose turn it was to clean, and we could invite people over at last. But does this mean we were suddenly happy? No. After forty-eight hours, we didn't even notice it. That problem was so last month. We just found something else to be irritated by (the slow Wi-Fi, the lack of

doors, the person who put the blueberry container back in
the fridge with only one blueberry). Humans adapt really
quickly to changed environmental conditions. We are on a
hedonic treadmill and cannot remain overjoyed. We quickly
forget how happy a change made us, no matter how we had
yearned for it.

Yes, our spouses should delight us. But delight is not
shelf stable like baked beans; it's like soufflé—amazing
while it lasts, but impossible to hang on to. We may have
longed to marry our partners, and dreamed of all the time
we would get to spend with them, but once we get to live
with them, we adapt and yearn for something else. We return, more or less, to the level of contentment we had before we married. People think marital bliss is like floating
down a river without a care in the world. They're right,
but only in that pretty soon, someone is going to get bored
or restless and decide to rock the boat.

Recently my husband was cooking while I was paying
bills in another part of our home. "Hey," he called out,
standing less than two feet from the pantry. "Do we have
any more peppercorns?" *Here's the thing about familiarity,* I reminded myself. *It's impossible to have family without it.* I went and found the peppercorns. They were in the
pantry.

CHAPTER 2

Fighting

One of the biggest stupid arguments I ever had with my spouse was about a barbecue. (To be clear, we've had bigger ones, but they were less stupid. And we've had stupider ones, but they were smaller, like a recurrent spat about why I always forget to put out butter when I'm setting the table.) The barbecue argument started because we don't have an oven in our home. We don't have an oven in our home because my spouse is an architect and an enthusiastic chef and not insanely wealthy, so it has been burdensome to find one that met all his design, culinary, and budgetary specifications. We make do with a stove top and a microwave. You can do almost anything with those, except make something for your kids' school bake sale. (Win-win!)

We don't have an oven, but we do have a deck. We have

a deck, because my spouse is an architect (I may have mentioned this?) and for my birthday one year he just decided to stick one out the back of our apartment in Manhattan, and somehow designed one that met all the necessary zoning/material/budgetary limits. I'll take a deck over an oven any day of the week. Soon afterward, it occurred to me that we could get a grill. He thought it was a great idea. Although first, he said, we'll need to run a gas line out there. So we'll need to get a plumber and remove some of the wall and maybe that affects the air-conditioning, hard to tell. I huffed that we could just go to the store and get a grill with a gas canister, since all that brick removal sounds like it would take at least as long as finding an oven. He counter-huffed that I never support his dreams. I pivoted and remarked that it was in fact *my* dreams that were being unsupported, or at least deferred indefinitely. Maybe I wept a tiny bit. We bought a gas canister grill. It was a huge pain, because you can't buy replacement gas canisters in Manhattan unless you're doing a job that requires using them. (Thanks again, Taliban!) After a year or two we threw out the grill (which was always out of gas) and installed one with a gas line.

I like to say: we were both right! He likes to say we solved that fight by spending $400 on something we only used for two years. If the kids are out of earshot, I then point out how much cash we've dropped on them and got no use out of them whatsoever. So we call that fight a draw. Or, at least, I do.

You and the person you adore will fight. Do not expect to not fight. People who don't fight are scary. Either their unions will not last because one of them is repressing a lot of feeling or has zero self-esteem, and those things will eat the marriage alive, or they are both cyborgs and the machine invasion has already begun. Marriage is all about fighting. This seems like a grim thing to say, but it's true. If you can't figure out how to disagree, you can't figure out how to be married. It's how you really learn what's important to you and to your spouse. It's how you understand what his or her real fears are. It's how you clarify what your own real fears are. We write marital quarrels off as little bumps in the road to be avoided or endured, when in fact they are key landscape features, to be watched and mapped and surmounted. Once you understand them, and navigate them, you will know so much more about the topography of your lover and yourself. You'll also have a rough outline of the least treacherous route forward for the partnership.

It's naïve to believe that two people could intertwine their lives, plot their futures, sleep in the same bedroom, wrangle their children, and figure out who's going to clean the fridge after the milk leaked onto the onions, without occasionally having divergent opinions. Most people couldn't manage it for a week, let alone a lifetime. The difference with fighting in a marriage and fighting in, say, a cage match is that you don't necessarily have to win. Marital melees are more like the stuff you see on Wrestle-Mania. A lot of the tension is not in the fisticuffs but in the players' backstory. And who wins actually matters less than an outcome that ensures that these two combatants will meet again.

On the face of it, I know, it feels like people who love each other should be able to disagree peaceably. After all, we all went to considerable effort to find The One and marry him or her. We sifted through a lot of individuals, often at great personal cost to our dignity and wallets, before landing on this one human with whom we got on better than anyone else. We had deep late-night conversations in which we felt profoundly understood or inspired. We discovered new things about ourselves and the world. Shouldn't we at minimum have found someone with whom we can agree most of the time?

Highly unlikely. And even if you did, that person will change. And so will you. Or they won't, even if you really want them to. You'll encounter situations you've never dealt with before and you will be stunned by how your natural reaction will be 180 degrees the opposite of your spouse's and how there will be no possibility of compromise. The way you deal with these discrepancies—from the tiny little tiffs to the enormous barn-burning withdraw-half-the-money-from-your-joint-checking-account brawls—will shape the course of your love, in the same way that a flood of water shapes the course of a river. It can make it burst its banks, carve out new territory, or form a nice deep groove.

Some therapists believe that what people disagree about—money, sex, kids, mess—is a lot less important than how they disagree. And studies[1] have shown that "conflict behaviors," which is sociological slang for the way people fight, are much more predictive of divorce than how rich you are, what kind of background you have, and what happens over the course of your life. John Gottman, the godfather of relationship research, says that he can put people in a room—he actually has a laboratory/apartment set up for this—watch them interact and ascertain with a pretty high degree of accuracy whether they will stay married or not. When people react to each other with contempt, criticism, stonewalling, and/or defensiveness—which he calls the Four Horsemen of the Apocalypse—they are likely doomed. (Other therapists give them different names but have identified similar behavior.)

"Irreconcilable differences," the go-to divorce option for the rich and famous, might more accurately be called "insufficiently developed fighting styles." We are all irreconcilably different. We just have to figure out how and what that means. The fight about the outdoor grill in our home has cropped up in our marriage in a thousand different permutations. Through them, I have learned that I like to get things done, even if they are a compromise. My husband will endure a lot of hardship for the result he wants. One way of saying this is that I am sloppy and he is rigorous. Another is that I am realistic and he is insane. Understanding that doesn't only mean that we have a decoder key for some of each other's behaviors, it means we've got a decoder key for ourselves.

But even self-knowledge doesn't prevent fights. Those still have to happen. They are a bit like taking out the garbage. Some people like to do a little bit of it every day, to keep the home spic-and-span. Others prefer to wait until they've got a jumbo-size Hefty sack of junk to purge and then have at it. Eventually we all have to roll up our sleeves and negotiate around, battle through, or settle with the deal breakers, so we can get to the fun parts.

A FAIR FIGHT IS A HARD FIGHT

Psychologist and therapist Stan Tatkin, who has developed a marital therapy technique known as PACT (Psychobiological Approach to Couples Therapy) and written a bunch of books about the brain and love, tells me there are only three things that prevent humans from settling our differences in a constructive way: we're useless at speaking clearly, our perception is lousy, and our memories are atrocious. "We could boil down most problems between people as truly built on misunderstanding," he says. "If you think your communication is good, then you're making more mistakes than you know. If you think your memory is accurate, you're completely wrong. And humans' sense-perception changes when we're threatened." A lot of people divorce when they don't need to, in his opinion, because they put too much faith in their own aptitude at these three skills: communicating, remembering, and interpreting. "If they only knew how fallible they are, and how many decisions are made based on these three, they would regret it because these are incredibly imperfect."

Tatkin believes it's not just what we're thinking, but how our bodies are reacting—our heart rate, our breathing, our limbic system—that is affecting our behavior with our spouses. He studies people by using digital frame analysis—he videos people and then watches faces and bodies and voices frame by frame. "We see over and over again how easy it is for people to misunderstand each other," he says.

If people perceive what's happening as threatening to them in some way—to their understanding of who they are, to the relationship, or even physically—they move into survival mode. Their inbuilt fight-or-flight response is triggered, that system by which humans instinctually react to threat, which means things can escalate fast. "This is something that amplifies very quickly between people without them understanding why," says Tatkin. "Before they know it, they're acting and reacting as if their partner is a predator. And that is the human condition. It's not a fault."

The trick with constructive fighting, then, is to remember that we have to be able to rumble while doing our best to keep the other person feeling safe. And, conversely, to remember that it's highly unlikely that our hitherto loving partner is suddenly a threat. (Unless, all joking aside, he or she really is. In which case, it's time to get out and seek some serious professional help.) An openhearted fighting stance—in which you overtly care for your partner, despite the current conflict—sounds simple in theory, but it's much harder to stay supportive in a heated moment than it is to imagine doing so. "I've seen far too many relationships end before their time because people cannot get this simple concept," Tatkin has said. "Our major job is to protect each other and make each other feel safe and secure."[2]

One of the sorest subjects in our house, for example is Lance Armstrong, the seven-time winner of the Tour de

France, the world's most famous cycling race. My husband loves the Tour. It's all his favorite things: visually arresting, technically complicated, and gratuitously punishing. For those who somehow avoided his story, Armstrong, a sinewy, frank-talking Texan, won the Tour more times than anybody else ever, from 1999 to 2005, after surviving metastatic testicular cancer. He came in third while recovering from a broken collarbone and once spent most of a day with his back wheel brakes engaged. He started a cancer charity and raised a reported $500 million for it. He dated a rock star for a while. The man could take some punishment.

Because road racing, as this type of cycling is known, has been historically quite prone to doping, people thought Armstrong must have been cheating. But he never failed a test. People in cycling circles sometimes claimed they had heard him admit to doping or had helped him cover up his doping, but he and those around him always pointed to the test results and said those people were crazy or jealous or unpatriotic or just vindictive and bitter.

But of course, he was doping. He admitted it to Oprah Winfrey on television in 2013 (because *all* the biggest cycling fans watch Oprah). He was a cheat and a liar and a bully who used his influence and power to silence and take down innocent people who spoke the truth. Everybody knows that. Even my spouse.

The fight between my husband and me is about whether Armstrong is nevertheless admirable. The man with whom I have thrown my lot argues that if everybody was doping in that era, then Armstrong was still the best athlete of all because everybody was getting the same advantage. I argue that his deceit and the destruction he wreaked on the sport and his viciousness toward people who outed him cancel every achievement. It wasn't just the act; it was the cover-up that was so egregious. He talks about all that Armstrong did for cycling and cancer. I talk about all the fans and associates he betrayed.

Clearly I'm right. But what makes this fight particularly vicious has nothing to do with cycling. I find my husband's support of Armstrong morally questionable. Does the man I love condone lying and intimidation? Does this mean he would lie to me? Does this mean he bullies people? Why are these behaviors so minimal in his eyes? My husband claims that he doesn't condone those things, he just doesn't think they erase Armstrong's athleticism or accomplishments. He can't stand the schadenfreude and the fair-weather fans.

The fight is not about Armstrong. It's about values and fears. I value honesty. The guy who gets to the top through deceit and intimidation is a villain to me. I fear deception. If my husband fails to be honest with me, I could get really hurt, our family could be destroyed, and whatever we have built up could be jeopardized. That's alarming. My husband, on the other hand, values loyalty and fears desertion. He abhors that people have turned on their erstwhile hero because he wasn't perfect. This might mean that if things get tough, or he makes a mistake, I will abandon him. To this day, nobody who knows us well brings up Lance Armstrong in our vicinity.

Given that some fights are deeply loaded (like the above), some fights are just the same fight you always have in a different setting (like our efficiency over quality spats), and some fights really are trivial (like the butter), how can you fight well? All warfare, according to Sun Tzu, is based on deception.[3] It follows then that marital fighting, in which we don't need a winner, but a truce, must be based on lack of deception. When you fight, fight fair. Don't threaten to divorce. Don't be shifty about what you want or what you did. Don't change your position just to win. If you think you can manage that, then there are still two strategies good fighters use. One is technique: how to handle the contretemps. The other is context: when and where to fight. (What is worth fighting about will be covered in subsequent chapters.)

WHEN YOU START IT

How can you tell if you're fighting in that WrestleMania way, where you don't actually hurt your partner but still arrive at a result, and not in the Ultimate Fighting way, which eventually leads to people tapping out of the marriage? The first hint is that you are starting a lot of sentences with "You," or even worse, the dreaded "You always" or "You never." [Cue sirens.] Some examples might be "You never put anything away," "You never want to have sex," or the dreaded "You always smell of cheddar." This is criticism, not problem-solving. You are making the person the problem rather than making the actual problem the problem. The person you're sharing your life with, having been insulted or wounded, is likely to be less inclined to work with you. Marital arguing 101 suggests that wherever possible, issues that need resolution should be approached with sentences that begin with "I." "I would love it if you could put your socks away" or "I've noticed a strange new smell, sort of cheesy. Have you?"

Sue Johnson, a psychologist and clinical therapist who specializes in an attachment science-based technique known as Emotionally Focused Therapy, calls the people who tend to begin fights with "you" accusations "blamers."[4] Other schools of therapy use the word *pursuers*. It's not that people who fight this way are particularly intemperate. Often they are merely making the most logical response to a given set of circumstances, which is that their concerns are going unheard. On just the second night of our honeymoon, my husband and I watched an old couple trying to reverse into a tricky parking spot. The wife was standing behind the car as the husband backed in. "No!" she screeched, waving her hands. "*This* way. Too *much*. Straighten *up*!" My spouse asked me why old ladies sounded like that. (He was nervous about his future.) "It's probably the only tone of voice she has left that he still responds to," I guessed. Like that lady, blamers are just doing what they can to get through to their partners. "Blamers speak of being alone, left, unimportant, abandoned, and feeling insignificant to their partner," says Johnson. "Underneath their anger they are extremely vulnerable." Arguers of this type are also known by a more colloquial name, especially if they're women, which they often are: nags. (Please note: I'm not endorsing this name, just defining it.)

One of the most difficult parts of arguing well is that often what feels right is altogether wrong. Everybody, for example, not just blamers, sometimes feels compelled to complain. They don't call it venting for nothing; it's incredibly satisfying to unstop a pressure valve of resentment you've built up over weeks or months or years and really let fly about your sufferings and how a person who promised to love you has caused them. It feels warranted. It feels healthy. It feels like we have a right to let people know just exactly what's going on in our neck of the woods.

But complaint, like criticism, does not open an avenue to dialogue and change. It merely strews the route with unsightly detritus. This is a tough one, because we denizens of the twenty-first-century Westernized cultures have been taught that repression is bad and expression is good. What is social media after all but a huge pulsating cloud of people saying exactly what they're exercised about? Yet if we've learned anything from a dozen years' worth of Facebook posts (or about twenty minutes of Tweets), it's that nobody changes his or her mind about anything after they've been insulted or compared to Hitler/Stalin/Lucius Malfoy.

So how do you make your needs known? Nearly all the therapists I spoke to or studied in the course of researching this book advise that brevity is a key virtue. Get in, make your point, get out. The quicker the better. "I haven't done a large-scale study," writes Harriet Lerner, a psychologist who specializes in relationships and women, "but my observations suggest that the higher the word count on an emotionally laden subject, the faster the other person shuts down."[5] Complaining can be a bit of a positive feedback cycle, in which you start to explain what's bugging you and explaining it makes you agitated, which then creates more distress. And that's just you. Your partner is also responding, which is also setting off its own reaction. Both criticism and complaint set up a chain reaction of negative call and response, what Tatkin describes as "a very fast-acting interaction where I started a little fire, but then I threw gasoline on it with you, and you threw gasoline on it with me, and now this is a full-fledged forest fire." Even the great military strategists agree with this. "There has never been a protracted battle," Sun Tzu writes in *The Art of War,* "from which a country has benefited."[6]

Terrence Real, a Boston-based psychotherapist and author of three bestsellers about marriage, has an interesting three-step technique for raising a problem with a partner called The Feedback Wheel that helps to keep things brief. It's an adaptation of techniques pioneered by the late therapist Janet Hurley, and refined by Real in his book *The New Rules of Marriage,* and it's pretty simple. First you have to do these completely obvious-sounding but nevertheless necessary things like asking your partner if he or she is willing to listen and then reminding yourself that you love this person. You then tell your partner four things:

1. What you saw or heard that you found problematic. Not "This is what you did . . ." but "This is what I saw . . ."

2. What you made up about it—that is, what you came to believe as a result of what you saw. You're supposed to literally say, "What I made up about this is . . ." This is a weird locution that ensures

that you are only talking about your impressions, not making assumptions.

3. How you feel about it.

4. How you'd prefer it go down next time.

And lastly, you let go of the outcome. Whatever happens, you thank your partner for listening and move on. Do not escalate.

As an experiment, I tried this with my spouse. The altercation I used had occurred when he was on an international call trying to help his eighty-three-year-old dad fix his slow computer, at the same time as I was arguing with a teenager about exactly how much Netflix was acceptable to watch on any given day. The teenager's voice was raised, my voice was raised, my husband lost it and hung up on his dad, then turned on us, and our house blew up like a bad news story. I thought he had behaved unfairly, since prior to the argument with our child, he had endorsed my plan for handling teenage screen habits.

So a day or so later, after rereading Real's technique, I asked my spouse if we could talk about something. He didn't run from the room, so I kept going. I explained what I saw (he went ballistic). I explained what I made up about that, although Real's words seemed preposterous, so I went with "What this led me to believe . . ." (he wasn't a loyal comrade in the battle against the invasion of the mind snatchers in our child's life). I said how it made me feel (bewildered and betrayed) and I said what I'd like (for him to take my side in this issue, since he'd already given it his blessing). This took about four minutes. Then it was his turn. I got a full multi-chapter lowdown on my flaws as a spouse, a parent, a woman, a human, a primate, and a mammal. The attention to detail was impressive, as was the endurance. Who knew somebody could talk this long on one subject without resorting to notes? At one point I was worried we'd need to break for refreshments. Finally he was done. And then, of course, according to the rules of this game, I was not allowed to say anything back, just to thank him for hearing me out. I *almost* did it, too.

While Dr. Real's technique seemed alarmingly one-sided to me, that issue did not ever come up again in our house. And it brings us to the hardest part of fighting well: listening.

WHEN YOUR PARTNER STARTS IT

I had a boss for several years who was quite deaf in one ear. His hearing got worse over the years, and doctors had told him that if he had been born with his hearing in this state, he'd have been classified as deaf. But most people didn't know. He used his one good ear, his natural intelligence, and close observation of the people with whom he was talking to compensate. When you were in conversation with him, he was not capable of doing anything but focusing on you. As a result, he was a great manager. People felt really *heard*. One of my colleagues, who didn't know he was deaf, called him a "power listener." Eventually he was promoted to a high-level position in the U.S. government and then a consultant to the heads of tech companies.

A lot of people are deaf around the person they're married to for other reasons. It's hard to hear the people we love telling us what's wrong with us. "There is no greater challenge than that of listening without defensiveness," says Harriet Lerner in *Why Won't You Apologize?*, "especially when we don't want to hear what the other person is telling us."[7] But we have to try; defensiveness is, as Gottman notes, one of those apocalyptic Four Horsemen.

Just as it sounds, defensiveness is when people respond to somebody else's question as if it were actually an attack. It's a tendency to take offense on any pretext. It can spring from guilt, frustration, shame, hostility, or just plain fatigue. And unfortunately, spouses can really quickly get into the habit of ascribing negative intentions to their partners' words and beginning counter-maneuvers for protection even when none is needed. Once we move into a protective mindset and focus on making sure we don't get hurt, it's much harder to be open to what our partners actually want to tell us. The things that keep dangers away also make us harder to reach.

An easy way to tell you're being defensive is if, when your partner says they're having a problem with something, your response implies that this is their fault/problem/illusion. An old chestnut from this school is the "I don't think we're going to be able to pay the X bill," which is met with any variant of the "What are you spending all the money on?/Do you think I'm made of money?/You think I don't know we don't have enough money?!/What are you talking about?" Nope. Wrong answers. You have just made large, unauthorized withdrawals from the goodwill bank and have tripped all the alarms around the safe. The person you're talking to, whom you love, now feels threatened. Fight or flight is now in effect. Good answers might be more along the lines of "Yikes. I wonder how that happened. What do you think we should do?" or "I know. I've been worrying about it. Do you have any ideas?" If you feel like you need to blame someone, you can always go with my standby, the U.S. Treasury Secretary, who as of this writing is Steve Mnuchin.

Sometimes, your spouse actually does do something stupid, mean, petty, or vicious; we're all human. In those cases, defensive reactions can progress all the way to retaliatory ones. This is often simply our reflexes at work, probably springing from the subcortical areas of our brain where actions that are deeply learned and require no thought originate. Here's how it works: your partner does something lousy and, before you know it, you've said or done something even more louse-ridden, and bingo, you're caught in a lousiness loop. Real has a great name for this; he calls it "offending from the victim position."[8] You see it in its purest form among toddlers. Little kid takes bigger kid's toy; big kid gives him a whack. But you see it in marriages, too: from insult-trading to the revenge affair. Retaliation is very cinematic; it's in all the great lovers' quarrels we see in movies: between Leonardo DiCaprio and Cate Blanchett in *The Aviator,* between Leonardo DiCaprio and Kate Winslet in *Revolutionary Road,* and between Leonardo DiCaprio and Margot Robbie (and a glass of water) in *The Wolf of Wall Street.* Leo does great retaliation.

Getting defensive and striking back can be appropriate responses when you are genuinely under attack. This is why those systems kick in, to help humans survive a predator or dangerous situation. But they are poor strategies to use on members of your own team. And when *both* spouses use them, there be dragons. In a longitudinal study[9] of seventy-nine young couples, so-called "negative reciprocity," in which each partner used those destructive behaviors on the other, correlated with their getting divorced within seven years.

One of the most persistent fouls in the marital boxing ring is scorn. It's usually comorbid with contempt, that toxic habit from the first chapter. Scorn has many forms: Repeating something somebody says in an annoying voice. Belittling their concerns. Exaggerating what they're talking about until it's preposterous. It doesn't even have to be verbalized. Body language will do nicely: the rolled eye, the turned head, the tone of voice, the crossed arms, the refusal to put down the personal communication device. All these gestures are dismissive: they convey the impression that the listener does not believe the speaker is communicating vital, new, or helpful information. They're such reflexes, sometimes people don't even realize they're doing them. "These very subtle, small things happen so quickly that if people aren't careful, they can cause a threat response, which will then continue and repeat and amplify," says Tatkin. "And then it becomes a biological matter that people will find very difficult to get out of."

The most robust breed of scorn can be found in relationships in which two people have already decided what they believe about each other—the negative sentiment override we saw in chapter 1—and register every interaction as further evidence that they are right. "A couple's repetitive fight remains unresolved because neither partner truly engages with the other, but rather with *his worst fantasy about the other,*" notes Real.[10] This default position is mutually exclusive, of course, with sorting anything out but is fantastic if you love rehashing old grievances and generating little new ones along the way.

THE PECULIAR CASE OF WITHDRAWAL

Often, but not always, the coping mechanism used by partners to deal with fights follows a gender type. Women, as noted above, tend to be blamers, who want to air a problem. Men tend to be withdrawers.[11] This is how that looks: Your partner-lover-spouse, whom for the purposes of this discussion we shall call the plaintiff, comes to you and you decline to litigate the issue. You don't put on a defense, you just sit there. Or as soon as the arguments are laid out, you leave. Perhaps you think the protest is without merit. Perhaps you've heard the person's charges a bunch of times before and you see no way forward. Perhaps the mention of it is so upsetting, you cannot bear to stick around and be blamed for it all once more. Or perhaps you feel guilty and just decide to go straight to a self-imposed solitary confinement.

Again, this fighting style has its roots in insecurity.

Johnson has noticed in her practice that "withdrawers speak of feeling ashamed and afraid of hearing that they are failures. They believe that they can never please their partner and so feel helpless and paralyzed." Always walking away, however, or constantly staying silent and refusing to engage can be just as damaging as retaliating. Nothing says "you are unloved" more than having your requests, anxieties, or desires for change utterly ignored.

When I first arrived in New York City, you could talk to taxi drivers. These days, there is a permanent Plexiglas shield between the front seat and backseat, so conversation is almost impossible. Also, there's Uber. But back in the day, taxis sometimes had an operable barrier between the driver and the passenger, which could move up or down. You could get to know your cabbie. I remember one whose opinions on the best way around Manhattan did not concur with mine. He ignored all my directions. Probably he felt that because he was the professional driver and I was an idiot, he should just go the way he wanted. To me, however, it seemed like I was the paying customer, so I got to choose the route. And that this guy was just another in a long line of men who discounted women's opinions. Galled at being so ignored, I devised a plan. When we got to our destination, before I paid him, I would let him feel my righteous anger. About three seconds into my lecture—I believe I had got as far as "You know, it's guys like you who give a bad name to taxi drivers . . ." when a thick, clear divider began to rise between us. It was a completely effective f*** you. I tipped him anyway, because I wanted to be the bigger person. And I am pathetic.

If you intend to have no further communication with the human soul you are shutting out, like my cabbie comrade, then declining to engage is a pretty good way to minimize your losses and go about your business. But if you're married, the raising-the-barrier approach must be used very carefully. You could end up in a siege, with someone throwing emotional grappling hooks to try to get to you. Several studies have found[12] that in young couples withdrawal was linked to divorce in fewer than seven years as problems went unresolved and distance and alienation grew between partners. One particularly depressing study[13] found that even if wives used constructive problem-solving techniques and husbands used withdrawal, they were more likely to divorce than not.

There is, however, an exception. Research[14] shows that while the withdrawal style is damaging in the early years of marriage, it doesn't seem to have the same effect on more seasoned duos. That might be because the folks in longer-lasting marriages have learned how to use the off-ramp in a more productive way. Instead of driving away completely, they pull over to the side of the road and take a break. Therapists suggest that it's okay to put a hold on an argument, as long as you let your partner know that you're not simply unilaterally exiting negotiations. Instead, you are taking a beat to process what they've said, or believe that moment in time is less than ideal for having this discussion (you have company or commitments elsewhere), or that you need to cool off and can continue the talk when you've calmed down a bit.

The key here is that you are not putting your other half on mute. You are hitting pause and will return. Some therapists even recommend a safe word, meaning a signal for a time-out. I read of one couple for whom putting on a funny hat indicated one of them needed a breather. They also suggest that, if possible, you actually schedule a time to pick up the subject, so the person you're living with knows that they will be heard. If the fight was a bruiser, though, you might want to give it at least a day and one good sleep.

WHEN TO FIGHT

I've always regarded with suspicion the classic old embroidered cushion motto that you should never go to bed angry. Why on earth not? Why should two people try to deal with a delicate, complicated, emotionally fraught situation when they are already tired and cranky? It's like we've learned nothing from all the hard work toddlers have put in to demonstrate the natural conditions around which a tantrum is most likely to occur. A 2017 study[15] backed up my suspicions. A bunch of newlyweds were asked about how well their marriages were going, and those who needed sleep gave a much darker evaluation of their situation. By all means go to bed angry, as long as you both are going to get some rest. Yes, even if this means you're each anchored to the far side of the bed, wearing pajamas for the first time in months, and plotting all the things you're going to say in the morning. Unless you really can't get to sleep (and I mean, after you've honestly tried for at least an hour), the conversation is going to be more civil and more rational in the morning light.

It took me an embarrassingly long time to realize that the man I married was vastly more reasonable when (a) he got a lot of sleep and (b) had eaten enough. My spouse's metabolism is like that of a muscle car: he runs hot, he needs regular outings to keep the engine purring, and he can run out of gas when you least expect it. So, occasionally, when we're having a fight that I'm bewildered by, I sneak in a question on whether he has eaten. More often I try to head it off at the pass. He loves cheese. Both he and I try to make sure there's a lot of cheese in the house. Some men come in from a hard day at the office and head for the drinks cart. My spouse prefers the dairy case. I know this sounds obvious, but even really smart people overlook it. I once asked Mark Zuckerberg, the chief executive officer of Facebook, how Sheryl Sandberg had changed the way things were done at the social networking giant, and he said that after Sandberg arrived, they were all less hungry. She made sure everybody in meetings was fed. Take it from one of the world's richest women: don't figure stuff out while hungry.

Another bad place or time to draw swords is while driving. For years, the car has been considered a great place to have a sensitive talk with a teenager, because nobody has to look at anybody, but partly for that same reason, it's not a great place to have it out with your spouse. Foremost, *somebody is driving,* which means they are already using—or should be using—quite a lot of their brain's bandwidth. Hashing out an emotional issue is very taxing on people's mental resources, and so you don't want to be needing those cognitive engines anywhere else. But according to therapists, that's not even the biggest problem. "The biggest problem," says Stan Tatkin, "is that we're legally blind on the sides of our eyes. We only see the world in high definition through a very small pinhole directly ahead of us." So you can't see the person you're trying to communicate with. You can't register what effect your words are having or get all the information on what they're really feeling. You can only hear them. And your anatomy makes things worse. "The amygdala, which is the fear center of the brain, fires more rapidly when a face is to the side," says Tatkin. "So I am more primed for threat with you at my side than if you were straight in front of me."

For similar reasons, trying to fight over text or over the phone is a fool's errand. For a start, it's super easy to lose it, forget yourself, and suddenly end up being the person screaming "I don't give a monkey's bottom what your brother thinks!" into a phone in a supermarket aisle. It's also more likely than not that you will misunderstand the intentions, tone, typing, emojis, or attitude of the person who is tapping out messages to you. This is another time when the stereotype of our spouse that we all carry around in our heads comes into play; we are apt to attribute certain meanings or intentions to his or her words that are unhelpful and wrong.

It's better to see people's faces and bodies when we have important fights with them. It's better to look right at them. We cannot fight with our lovers in the same way we fight our foreign enemies: from far away in bunkers, with drones and air strikes, pushing buttons on a screen. That may be an effective way to win a war, but it is no way to negotiate a truce.

Don't fight when you're on a date. If you've scheduled a night out with your significant other, just to have fun and check in and give yourself the chance to be reminded of all the things that made that person seem so sparkly to you in the first place, then don't try to sort your crap out. That's like doing your taxes at the amusement park. Get your good-times ledger in the black. Don't pollute your fun with duty.

There's some disagreement in the academic and therapeutic circles about whether you should fight in front of the kids. Generally the rule is that it's okay to haggle stuff out with your fellow parent if the fight is not too bruising and you're playing by the rules, attacking the issue, not the human. It's actually useful for them to see how people who love each other negotiate. Research has found,[16] for example, that one of the reasons kids from divorced families get divorced more often is that they have not observed how a fight can be productive. They didn't have any tools or models for dealing with conflict except the instinctual, more animal ones. On the other hand, if the battles start to achieve high levels of conflict, or look like they're heading that way, you might want to, as they say, get a room. Also, kids don't need to hear you feuding over adult stuff like money or sex. And obviously, if you're fighting about the kids in front of the kids, unity is more important than justice.

After the fight comes makeup sex, which is totally a thing and I recommend it. But before then, you have to get through the next part, saying sorry. "Recovery," as therapists call the making-up part, is a skill that few marriages survive without. "The people who are the fastest at repairing injuries, the best at managing distress in the quickest way, are going to be the most successful couples by far," notes Tatkin. "The ones who stay in distress and can't repair or can't get out of it as a team are going to have the most trouble because the longer we're in a state of mind, the longer we're dealing with an experience that was negative, the more likely it goes into long-term memory."

WHEN YOU'RE THE ONE
WHO NEEDS TO SAY SORRY

Here's the curious thing about apologies. What else are we taught to do from a young age that we still suck so much at as adults? We master walking upright, talking, the pincer grip, comic timing, and fiddly workarounds when one function of our smartphone stops working. Many of us know when to write *it's* and when to write *its*. (It's not that hard once you understand its different forms.) But we still completely botch saying sorry. Hardly anybody gets it right, especially when talking to the folks for whom it means something.

The first lesson in apologies is that they don't hurt and

they usually help. So make them. They come much more easily with practice, so make them often. Be liberal. When your spouse or partner has a beef with you, the easiest way to defuse it is to figure out if you can apologize for it. Is there a specific transgression you can identify for which you can take responsibility and endeavor to not do again? Cut that quarrel off at the pass.

Some U.S. researchers measured mathematically whether quick apologies are more effective than tardy ones. Their answer: "By interpreting the logarithmic function as the result of a process of decay plus a process of consolidation, it seems to follow that interventions for influencing forgiveness might be most effective if they are administered relatively early after transgressions have occurred because relatively little consolidation will have occurred at that point in time—just as the formation and decay of memories can be best influenced by processes that occur early in time after initial learning occurs."[17] In other words, yes. If you apologize quickly, the offense doesn't move from the short-term memory into the region of the brain where more solid recollections are formed. The aggrieved party doesn't get to stew over it.

The second trick with apologies is to remember why you're making them. Not to make you feel less guilty. Not to make the other person feel better or, worse, to shut them up. It's to rebuild a bridge that you helped blow up, to reestablish communication, to try to hit restart on a relationship for which the screen has frozen. So keep them pure. Apologize exactly for what you did wrong. And then stop. Do not, for the love of mercy, add a "but." A but is an apology assassin. "I'm sorry I killed your cat but he lay in front of my lawnmower" or "I'm sorry I didn't pick up the phone but you had already called me seven times." These are not apologies. Don't even bother with them. These are explanations/excuses. They communicate no sorrow, responsibility, or willingness to alter your course. You can explain your actions, but leave that for another time, after you have reestablished a connection.

In my house's longest-running battle, then, there is no point in my saying "I'm sorry I didn't put butter on the table, but you're the only one who eats it and I'm pretty sure it's bad for you." This does not help. Trust me, I already tried it.

The only thing worse than an apology with an appended "but" is the apology with the added "if." No. No. No. This is an insult. This is patronizing. "I'm sorry if you felt hurt." "I'm sorry if what I said came out the wrong way." "I'm sorry if my apology was no good." What you are actually saying here is "In the unlikely event that you are right and I have unwittingly done some trivial thing wrong, then, well, my bad." Nobody who has gone to the trouble of explaining to you what is upsetting them is going to be satisfied by that response because it lacks the prime apology ingredient: remorse. When you add an "if" to your apology, you are declining to acknowledge any fault. "I'm sorry if you wanted butter on the table" is simply not going to cut the margarine.

The only time you can offer an "if" apology is, of course, when you're not sure you've done anything wrong and you're trying to find out. "I'm sorry if I stepped on your toe in that commotion." Or "I'm sorry if I made that meeting more difficult than you had hoped." When somebody has already explained their beef, the "if" train has left the station.

Apologies don't work if the other person doesn't feel that they were listened to, that their anger and pain have been noticed. Harriet Lerner urges people to be "deeply curious" about the hurt person's experience. "If only our passion to understand the other person were as great as our passion to be understood," she writes.[18] By really listening to people, we can identify with precision what we did wrong and more accurately articulate what we are apologizing for. A key indicator to people that they have been heard is that our apologies focus solely on their wounds and not on what we want, like forgiveness or an acknowledgment that they were partly to blame.

If you really can't figure out who is in the wrong, or the unraveling will take too long and you need the fight to be over before, say, the guests start arriving for Thanksgiving, you can employ the useful phrase "I apologize for my part in this fight" and then try to figure out what that is from there. In most cases, however, an apology is a couture product. It can't be formulaic or store-bought. If you've addressed exactly your trespasses or oversights and communicated genuine personal dismay about them, the third part of an apology is to offer some evidence of a course correction. "I'm sorry I neglected to put butter on the table yet again. I have a blind spot about it. I'll do my best to remember it in the future." This is a speech that, as of this writing, I have never made.

If you make a real doozy of a transgression, it's a good idea to carefully choose the time and a place to express regret. It's not fake to give this some forethought. Wise generals, Sun Tzu notes, make the mind of their opponent their first consideration. So spend a moment assessing when your partner might be in the best frame of mind to hear you out and schedule your sorry accordingly. Just don't let that be another excuse for putting it off or chickening out altogether.

How do you help your aggrieved lover forgive you after you've apologized? The best way is to preempt the mistakes you are going to make by building a good relationship with your partner before you're in the doghouse. Research shows that people more readily forgive people whom they trust.[19] But if that ship has already sailed, then you need to restock the trust fund by showing that you are attempting to set things right. Author and clinical psychologist Janis Abrahms Spring calls this "the transfer of vigilance."[20] That is, when you have done something awful to your partner—insulted them in public, spent hard-earned savings without telling them, been unfaithful—you need to be as vigilant as they are that it won't happen again. That could mean complimenting your spouse in public or making sure you are ridiculously transparent in all of your financial affairs and/or interpersonal dealings with the opposite sex, or same sex, if that's your jam. But it mostly means being as observant of, and tender with, your lover's sore spots as you are with your own.

Finally, do not expect absolution straightaway, unless you are married to the pope (in which case, you have bigger problems than how to fight). You cannot force people to forgive you. You can only lay out the welcome mat. It's up to them to wipe their feet.

WHEN YOU'RE THE ONE
WHO'S HEARING SORRY

I was brought up in a family that is aggressive and competitive, but only in areas that don't matter. We are pussycats at negotiating for better pay or a promotion or in any kind of organized athletics; the gloves will come off, however, for board and beach games. These are serious. Nobody in the Luscombe tribe gets a break, no matter how young or elderly or frail or new to the family. And, yes, there is trash talk. I want you to remember that context when you read the following story: I was playing a game of cards (I believe it was Oh, Hell!) with my three brothers in one of our rare get-togethers. We were at that phase of life when the infrastructure we had rigged up in our youth was beginning to crumble. Setbacks in health, in family, in careers. My oldest brother had already divorced. My youngest was going through one. Perhaps because of this, he was taking too long to play. Consistently. Violating our unofficial family motto, *A fast game is a good game*. "Oh, for goodness' sake, can you please play?" I said. "You take so long, even I'd divorce you."

Needless to say, this joke did not land. This joke was never going to land. This joke should never have taken off. He got up and left. My other two brothers looked at me with open astonishment, tinged with what seemed like pity, the sort of look you might give an old lady who had just kicked a wounded baby koala. They didn't say anything, either. I vaguely remember thinking that what I said was too awful even for an apology. But I tried to say sorry and have said it again since. My brother works for the church, so he is pretty well versed in the theory of forgive-ness. And it turned out he wasn't too bad at it in practice, either. He did not dismiss the event. He did not minimize it or say it didn't hurt. He did not let me feel like it was in any way understandable, or humorous, or that he was fine with it, but he did not let it sever our relationship.

Forgiveness is actually a very simple process. It merely requires you to *forgo giving* people what they deserve. Like canceling a debt. Cleaning up the mess someone else made in your room. Declining to press charges. But pro-cesses that are simple are not necessarily *easy*. By some definitions, giving birth is simple: mothers merely squeeze another human being through a part of their bodies that's normally the circumference of a pool hose.

And as with delivering a baby, the prospect of forgiving someone may horrify us. Actually confronting a real hurt done to us—as opposed to insisting that it doesn't matter—and choosing to let it go is painful. It feels wrong and scary. Yes, we forgive our children all the time. We forgive our bosses and colleagues a lot, too. When we get old enough, we can usually manage to pardon our par-ents. Forgiving a spouse is one of the chewiest of the vari-etals, though. When the person you've chosen does you wrong, it's hard to swallow.

To get to the place where we even consider the option, it's helpful to realize that forgiveness is not primarily about a feeling. You don't have to want to do it. It's an act of will. A 2014 study[21] of more than three hundred college students who had recently been wronged found that people forgive more quickly if they feel less at risk of being hurt again by the person who did them wrong. This is why apologies and conciliation efforts work; they demonstrate that the intention toward the other person is not bad, that the mistake was a blip, not a pattern. But that and other studies[22] also showed that forgiveness was accelerated if the relationship was important to people and held future promise. This implies an element of choice. The students had some agency in their willingness to pardon. You can opt to forgive someone. It doesn't have to come naturally.

In the same way, forgiveness is not passive. It's a choice made at a cost. Forgivers are sacrificing one of their primary forms of deterrence. It can feel like they're inviting the perpetrator to wound them again, because they're not enforcing the penalty. An intimate partner can be particularly tough to absolve because the nature of the relationship means that he or she has many opportunities to re-offend. On the other hand, partners are all also high-value friends, so forgiveness is worthwhile. Absolution is one of those rare practices endorsed both from the pulpit and the laboratory. Some researchers and anthropologists argue that humans are good at exoneration because evolution dictates it; natural selection favors those who forgive their close relationship partners because it keeps them breeding and thus their genes are more likely to survive.[23] People of faith put it more poetically, observing that "love keeps no record of wrongs."[24] Whatever rationale you choose for exercising forgiveness is fine. Relationships don't survive without it. The only exception here is in the case of physical danger for you or your family. That's always a case for the professionals. Put this book down, pick up your phone, and call the domestic violence hotline or the police or a professional counselor now. A single incident doesn't always mean the end of the relationship, but it must not go ignored or untreated.

A lot of the folksy sayings about forgiveness center on how it is the gift you give yourself. "Why would you let people who did you wrong rent space in your head?" is one version. Or: "Holding on to a grudge is like drinking poison and expecting the other person to die." And it's true that not forgiving someone, especially for a very serious violation like cheating, can give the person who did you wrong a lot of power over your emotional life. But those cheery sayings underestimate how excruciating it can be to willingly quell your anger.

Most of the hard work of forgiveness is done in the first three months after the misdemeanor takes place. After that period, according to one study[25] of 372 college students, an aggrieved person is usually one-seventh as angry as they were right after the offense. But the same study also predicted that the forgiveness rate slowed to a trickle after that. Some scientists[26] theorize that forgiveness and forgetfulness might use similar cognitive processes, but this does not mean that forgiving is the same as forgetting. It simply means that the crappy thing your spouse did to you no longer has the power to wound you. Scars don't go away, they just stop hurting so much.

If forgiveness is proving particularly difficult, research[27] has shown that writing about the transgression and the lessons people learned in the course of recovering from their injury, even for twenty minutes a day, helped the process along. This was not—despite how it sounds—a Pollyannaish scrapbooking thing, but a way of engaging the victim's cognitive skills to help work through the process of overcoming the desire for retaliation, wanting to end the rift, and creating goodwill for the partner. This doesn't mean you have to understand why or accept that your partner treated you badly. It just means you have accessed your capacity for grace.

Grace is the goal, even when you're pretty sure you're right. Old-school journalists like me are very big on fact-checking and double-checking. Many of us were taught a motto in our earliest days as newsroom cubs: if your mother says she loves you, check it out. If you imagine that this might make us less fun to argue with, then you are correct. Being right is what we prize. Many is the time my husband has been halfway through a story when I have interrupted to ask for a source on a particular detail. He *loves* it. But there are occasions when being right is not—and I cannot believe I'm writing this—the most important thing. An insistence on arguing a point until everybody agrees with you every time is boring, annoying, and counterproductive. I am never going to admire Lance Armstrong. I have been at the same party and gone out of my way not to meet him. My spouse is always going to support him and has stood in the sun for more than an hour just to see him at a distance. We are not going to agree. At some point, that's got to be as good as it gets. Insisting on your judgment, your route, your memory of events, your technique, your method for installing a grill is a fool's errand.

As I was writing this book, I got an invitation for two to an early screening of the Academy Award–winning film *Icarus,* about Russia's doping program. Afterward there was to be a discussion about doping and its effect. And who was on the panel? Mr. Doping Expert himself, Lance Armstrong. Even though we knew we were risking some epic domestic turbulence, my husband and I went. And we survived. Afterward I told him I thought Armstrong actually made some pretty decent points. "Yeah, maybe," he said. "But he didn't look that fit."

CHAPTER 3

—

Finances

My mother is an heiress. The day that World War II was declared, her family moved from Belgravia in London to one of those stately homes in the English country where the address is just three words: House name, Village name, County name. In her case it was Meredith, Tibberton, Gloucestershire. My family visited it once, and as we approached, one of my brothers and I were remarking on its adorability. My mother interrupted us to note crisply that we were admiring the gardener's cottage.

The house was hidden down a long hedge-lined driveway. The owners showed us around. The orangery was still there, and the walled gardens, and the enormous music room. The bells downstairs had numbers corresponding to upstairs rooms, so the servants knew who had pressed the button signaling readiness for breakfast. My mom pointed out the high windows where she and her siblings used to throw water on each other, avoiding the less-well-off kids they took in during the blitz, as they all rode bikes around the house. Family legend had it that in between my ancestors and the current occupants it had been an asylum, which seemed like a change in occupancy hardly any of the neighbors would have noticed. But we learned during that visit that it had been more of a rehab facility for alcoholics, which, my brother and I agreed, wouldn't have been that different, either. Anyway, the place was huge. After the visit we had just one question for our mother: *What happened to all the money?*

My father, on the other hand, grew up in the Australian countryside. He was born during the Depression; his father was a bank manager. They lived in a house attached to the bank, since farmers don't really keep bankers' hours. His formative years were spent watching his dad deal with people struggling to hang on to their farms or to get the bank to lend them enough money to plant crops or feed sheep or hire shearers or care for their children.

His mother died young, and his father remarried. One day he announced that instead of finishing high school, my dad, Billy, was going to work as the office boy with an accountant acquaintance. Billy didn't understand at the time, but a year later my grandfather was dead (which his doctors had predicted), and my father was left to fend for himself and his stepmother. After paying for food, board, transport, and clothes, my dad said that if he saved, he could afford a milkshake once every two weeks. He used to hand-deliver letters near his lodgings so he could keep the tuppence his company provided for stamps.

After a lifetime of rotten luck, Billy got a break. He was drafted. He did his national service in the Australian Air Force's marine unit, training to rescue pilots who ended up in the ocean or assist seaplanes in distress. All of his food, accommodation, clothes, and transport were provided. And when he left the service after six months, he found that his patriotic—or absentminded—employer had continued to pay him. With the first savings he'd ever had, he traveled to Europe and on his way home, on the good ship SS *Orontes*, he met my mother, who was on the initial leg of a world tour. Her diary records: "I met a rather vulgar Australian who picks his teeth with his serviette." My father is no gold digger, but winning her over was possibly the shrewdest financial move he ever made.

Unsurprisingly, my dad is incredibly frugal. I'm not talking prudent; I'm talking ascetic. At eighty-five, he still wears at least one shirt he was given for his twenty-first birthday. (It was originally terry cloth, but over the intervening six decades he has patched it with old towels, of more or less the same color.) Some people have favorite chairs or books; my dad has a favorite piece of rope.

When the heiress married the miser, there were bound to be some interesting transitions. My mother likes fast cars, my father favors cheap ones. My mother loves fine dining and the theater, while my dad prefers to spend his leisure time scraping the extra apple off the peel or gnawing at the heart of a cabbage. My mother suspected there would always be enough money. My father suspected there would never be. Neither of them was right. They fought about money, but they kept it in perspective. They had separate accounts. My father gave my mother every second paycheck. They agreed upon who would pay for what. And at Christmas and birthdays they gave each other presents that they would have wanted. That's how one year my dad got a painting, even though he doesn't really like art, and my mother got a mulcher, even though she doesn't really like leaf litter.

I didn't understand what they saw in each other until, somewhat unexpectedly, a postdoctoral student at the Wharton School of Economics explained it. Scott I. Rick[1] advanced the theory—and found some proof—that spendthrifts might be drawn to tightwads to militate against their own tendencies. It turns out that the free-spender/frugal marriage my parents had is quite common. "The more people [are] dissatisfied with their own emotional reactions toward spending, the more likely they [are] to be attracted to a mate with opposing emotional reactions toward spending," Rick wrote in 2009. It's possible my parents got together not despite their financial backgrounds but partly because of them. (There are two flaws in this theory. One is that my parents don't concur with it. My mother likes to say that my dad married her for her fortune and her legs, it's just that the fortune held out a little longer. And the other is that the unions Rick studied often did not last; my parents have been together for sixty years.)

WHY MONEY MATTERS SO MUCH

Everybody comes into marriage with one important relationship they cannot end: the one they have with money. It's a deep, complicated liaison with a lot of history and often goes unacknowledged. As one of the ancient texts says: where your treasure is, that's where your heart will be. Money is not just currency. It comes with emotions attached. "There's a lot of internal feelings related to money because money can also reflect the power and the balance of the relationship," says Lauren Papp, the director of the Couples Lab at the University of Wisconsin, Madison, and author of several studies on marital conflict. "Money is something that we bring with us from our childhood. So, what does money mean to a person? If someone buys something, is that an act of love, is that an apology, is that just what you expect?" Managing the triangulation of the relationship with a spouse and with moola can be a very tricky business. Sometimes, to paraphrase Princess Diana when her husband, the future king of England, was cheating on her, the marriage can get a bit crowded.

Fights about money, therefore, are not just about having enough and sharing it equally; they strike at the essence of people's fears and hopes and desires. Fears of being alone and being destitute are intertwined; marriage and wealth both offer a sense of protection and a safe harbor. It's no accident that people who are under financial pressure get divorced much more often than people who aren't. It's also not a coincidence that people often delay getting married until they feel financially secure, which is one of the reasons why there has been a huge drop in marriage rates among those with a high school education or less, and why college graduates get married later, once they have found their footing.

Studies[2] have shown that money is the most commonly reported squabble-starter for couples (followed by kids, although that order is reversed for stepfamilies) and the source of the most heated arguments.[3] And in homes where money is not the most common cause of fights, it's still the fight that either lasts the longest or in which the same issues just keep coming back without getting resolved.[4] Finance fights, unlike others, often get more heated over time. In Papp's study, which got one hundred wives and one hundred husbands to keep a diary of all the fights they had over a two-week period, with detailed descriptions and ratings for each fight, husbands and wives reported feeling more depressed after money fights than after other fights and husbands reported feeling angrier during those spats than others.[5] Money is also the issue that most couples say is an external problem for them, that is, not one caused within the partnership but by an outside pressure. It's the number one reason, for example, that many people who live together say they don't get married.[6]

There are many plausible explanations for why finances are the spark that sets off the most blazing rows. The first is that the subject just comes up often. It's unavoidable. There are bills every month. If they don't get paid, the effect is immediate and difficult to ignore. So couples have plenty of opportunities to discuss who is going to pay for what, whether certain expenditures were prudent or necessary, and the root causes of that annoying gap between cash going out and cash coming in. The good news is that this means lots of chances to practice having these conversations in a coolheaded manner. The bad news is that this also means lots of opportunities for sphincter-tightening conversations full of accusations and finger-pointing.

Second, money crises can hit unexpectedly, which ramps up everyone's stress levels nicely. The broken-down car, the job loss, the child who suddenly needs medical help or therapy, the dead refrigerator with its warm beer. Financial setbacks also have a vicious way of cascading. You don't have quite enough money to fix a taillight, so you get pulled over and get a ticket. You don't have enough money for the ticket, so you get a fine. You can't make your full credit card payments for a few months, so the interest starts to compound.

Third, money fights are the ones that couples tend to put off. They then have to have that same fight about that same problem with overspending or failing to mention an expenditure or that unpaid bill or why we can't go away on spring break again and again and again. As Ada Calhoun writes in her terrific book *Wedding Toasts I'll Never Give,* in every marriage there will come a time when "you'll find yourself wistful for the days when you had to pay for only your own mistakes." Calhoun's husband occasionally missed planes with nonrefundable tickets. My husband occasionally misses credit card payments, even when we have the funds to pay them. There's nothing like a fight that you've already had six times this year to really get that blood boiling.

Because of that whole mixed grill, many, many financial discussions are not taking place under the most optimal conditions. It's hard to keep one's voice on an even tone when it's dark out and you have no electricity, or to be chill when your car got towed for not paying a fine and you're already working at two jobs to pay the bills. These are difficult conversations under the best of circumstances, and they're often taking place under really crappy ones.

Financial battles are also different from any other kind of feud, because the loss of money, or even the hint of an absence of money, provokes our strongest emotion: fear. People get depressed if they think their sex lives are going down the drain, but they don't panic. They get frustrated when they can't agree on how to discipline the kids or on who's doing all the childcare, but they don't start imagining that they're going to lose everything. Having somebody else take or control your money, on the other hand, feels existential. It's threatening. Intimate partners entrust each other with a lot of financial information and power; with a few clicks of a keypad or a forged signature, that person can get it all. Therapists call this kind of monkeying with money "financial infidelity" because it gets at a lot of the same trust issues as sex. If your spouse uses your joint earnings in a way that you find risky, it's very hard to stop the sirens in your head from sounding the alarm that signifies This Is Critical and Not a Drill.

That tight little ball of dread at the center of our marital fiscal discussions often tips us over into the irrational, as we imagine we could be left with nothing, walking the streets in ill-fitting shoes, dragging our belongs in a rolling suitcase with only one working wheel. There's a terror that we will have to leave where we live and the life we have, that our friends will desert us and the only people who will ever call us will be bill collectors. Partners who have access to our money, or who are our only source of money, can destroy us. That's a high-level worry.

THE MISTAKES MONEY MAKES US MAKE

This might be as good a time as any to tell you about the last time I lost $70,000. It's a hilarious story: I forgot to claim stock options. They expired. One day I had $70,000 waiting to be claimed and then about a month later when I realized I had forgotten to click on the "exercise trade" button on my computer, poof, the opportunity had gone. It's hard to describe the feeling exactly. I imagine you could replicate the effects by lying on the ground and having a friend drop a bowling ball on your abdomen from atop a stepladder. There's a little shock, some confusion, pain, nausea, and a profound wish that this had happened to somebody else. For a while, it hurts to breathe. The closest memory I could associate it with was when as a young girl I had tried to make Jell-O in a mold like the picture on the package. I hadn't waited long enough (the irony) and when I turned the Jell-O mold over, the not-quite-set dessert had slithered in a single blob out of the mold, off the plate, down the draining board, into the sink, and down the drain. I watched. I might have even clawed uselessly at the Jell-O, much as I pathetically called my benefits department, to see if there were some way I could get the money back. I had made something, it was there, but through sheer incompetence, it was gone. And it was All. My. Fault.

So, here's the dilemma facing a person in my position. Do you tell your spouse? Technically, that is also his money, marital property and all that. And it's not like the amount wouldn't have made a difference. Like many of our peers in the knowledge industries, we live what a friend described as a high-end hand-to-mouth existence. We make what seems like a decent amount of money yet never have any left over at the end of the month. But, again, technically, this windfall never really existed. I did not take away $40somethingthousandaftertax from him. I just failed to provide it. Stock options are not a big topic of discussion in our household (obviously), so he probably would never even know. How could it hurt to never mention it?

Complicating matters a little was the fact that this was not the first time I had cost us cash through sheer stupidity. When we were new immigrants to New York City with no jobs and two friends and just a few months of marriage behind us, I surrendered $60 to a three-card monte game on the streets of Chinatown. At the time that was probably 20 percent of our liquid assets. After we—sorry, I—lost it, my husband didn't say much, but there was an unspoken agreement between us that I was a moron.

Unlike me, my spouse did not grow up without money worries. This is a guy who still has issues with his toes because he didn't want to tell his parents, who struggled to make ends meet, that his school shoes were too small. He requires a taster for any already opened dairy beverage because he consumed too many glasses of spoiled milk in his youth. Economic hardship in childhood has been shown[7] to have adverse effects way into adulthood, both psychological and physical, and a money setback can trigger any number of nasty memories. I had no desire to fire off an emotional howitzer in my husband's vicinity. Plus, according to the financial security company Experian's figures, 20 percent of people who divorce say finances were a major factor.[8] Yikes.

My husband was friends with a couple, now divorced, who had a problem because the guy was in the habit of going out for groceries and coming back with new boots or a kayak. It seemed so random and selfish and thoughtless, but behind it was a more complex story. He was a refugee from Eastern Europe. His father, who had been a successful artist before the family fled, had to make his living working with his hands in his new country, and things were always a bit tight. Nobody in the family spoke English and they felt like aliens. This guy was so accustomed to delaying gratification, to surviving in dire situations, that buying things on impulse was his way of feeling like he belonged and was safe and in control. But for his wife, whose big family had relied on frugality and prudence to pay their bills and, although not wealthy, had opened their home to other kids, it was wasteful, unpredictable, and selfish. She felt that if he loved her, he would stop. She grew resentful and scared. He felt resentful and trapped. They couldn't get past it.

But we don't have to have had a deprived childhood to have money mess with our relationships. Studies have shown that wanting money and having money can both have a less than friendly effect on people's feelings for other people. In a fascinating series of experiments[9] in 2006, a group of American and Canadian researchers found that people who were reminded of cash by solving a puzzle that was about money or by having Monopoly money in their line of sight were then less likely to offer to help in situations where they were needed. They also took longer to ask for help to do tasks that were impossible to do alone. Money, it seemed from this experiment, made people feel more self-sufficient, but it also made people believe that others should be self-sufficient. Neither of these is a good precondition for marriage, the ultimate team sport.

More pointedly, several other studies have shown that people who are very materialistic—that is, who value having a lot of really nice stuff—simply report having less happy marriages.[10] In 2015, Singaporean researchers got two sets of people to imagine themselves shopping on a luxury street or going for a beautiful walk, after which they measured their attitudes toward marriage. Those who had imagined shopping had a more negative attitude toward getting married and having kids right afterward than the nature walkers.[11] They tested this six or seven different ways and came up with the same results. The researchers suggested that perhaps because materialism fosters a competitive outcome and not a cooperative one, and because it requires time and energy to accrue things, materialism "may orient users away from forming close relationships with potential marriage partners."[12]

Moreover, as anybody who has spent time in the company of the well-heeled or has trained in interpersonal theory knows, deprivation is relative. If people are getting by fine financially, but not as lushly as they had hoped, or not as lushly as their colleagues, neighbors, or former roommates, it can be a source of considerable anguish. Casting about for solutions as to why they are not doing as well as their peers, they land upon their spouses as a likely suspect.[13] One 2017 study[14] across several U.S. states found that husbands' negative perceptions of their wives' spending habits, whether they were based in fact or not, were almost as likely to cause money arguments as actual financial difficulties.

MONEY IS A MANY-GENDERED THING

The effect of wealth on marriage gets really interesting in an era where women have more economic power than ever. For a start, there are plausible arguments that women simply choose to get married less often when they don't need a provider. Single women who win the lottery are 6 percent less likely to get married in the next three years.[15] As much as 20 percent of the decline of marriage in the last thirty years can be attributed to the narrowing of the wage gap between men and women, according to a study out of the University of California, Davis.[16] And certainly women have opted to leave marriages a lot more as female earning power has risen. Figures suggest that two-thirds of divorces are now initiated by wives.

In my parents' day, the home-keeping business agreement was clear, if onerous. The men were supposed to provide the capital and the women were supposed to provide the labor. Most of the money my mother brought into the marriage my father undertook to steward. Her contribution did not give her a break on the housekeeping. Even when she went back to college and to work, she still did most of the chores and childcare. My dad was more of the handyman type.

But the rising economic power of women has changed so much about the way we earn and use and think about money. In the last thirty-seven years, the percentage of wives whose jobs pay them more than their spouses' jobs do has increased from about 4 percent to almost 25 percent,[17] and a dual income is considered by many to be more of a necessity to cost-neutral family functioning than an anomaly. In 2015, for the first time, according to the Institute for Family Studies, marriages in which the wife was more educated were more common than those in which the husband was. Those are huge shifts that lead to very different negotiations and attitudes to money within couples. Most of us either don't have a model from our parents on how to handle the issue or don't like the model we saw.

A generation of women who grew up watching their mothers ask their fathers for money—or struggle to find work and money after a divorce—are now much more likely to be proactive about having their own nest egg. In the course of researching this book I asked more than two hundred people how they organized their finances with their spouses. Their answers varied, but it was clear that many of the wives were wary of being dependents. "When I was 13 in 1973, I read [the feminist bestseller] *The Female Eunuch*," said Maggie Alderson, a respondent from Britain. "It put the idea in my head that I might someday have to ask a man for money to buy a dress. I swore in that moment that I would always have my own money that was not shared with anyone else."

While on the whole the increased earning power of women has been a total score for men, who, not unlike my dad, increased their income without having to increase their workload merely by marrying the right women, it has had its costs. Studies[18] have suggested that men who earn less than their wives are more prone to infidelity and more prone to use medication for erectile dysfunction. A recent Danish study—from a region of the world known for its progressive views on gender no less—found a 10 percent increase in the use of ED medication among couples in which women earned slightly more than their husbands.[19] It also found that wives who earned more or even equal amounts were more likely to be taking antianxiety medication. Research economists at the U.S. Census Bureau reported in 2018 that couples in which wives earned more than husbands tended to minimize the difference when reporting their incomes on census forms.[20] Wives were more likely to understate their income and husbands to overstate theirs.

Why? Researchers suggest that it's because men are struggling with the idea that they're not providers. For centuries, the male partner's job has been to bring home the goods—and it's probably still the model today's husbands grew up under—so when they don't or can't, they feel like they are failing, specifically as a male. Even in the twenty-first century, research shows, one of the ways men signal "mate quality," as they say in zoology, or draw in potential lovers, is to spend money.[21] Splashing around some cash is the human equivalent of fanning out your peacock feathers or sticking out your tortoise neck. So any setback in this area can lead to a loss of confidence in the bedroom, hence the Viagra, or a desire to reassert their alpha-ness, hence the affair, with all its reassurances that they are still attractive and virile. Wives, meanwhile, are walking on eggshells, trying not to provoke their husbands' feelings of shame but at the same time needing occasionally to bring up money, hence the antianxiety meds.

Comparison is the thief of joy, and he's also a freeloader in marriages. Partners often judge themselves by how they're doing relative to their spouses. (If you've been doing this in secret, relax, there are studies showing it's completely normal.[22] Yes, especially about income.[23]) The good news is that not all men have been unsteadied by the perception that their wives are doing better than they are on the provider front, especially younger men. An analysis[24] of twenty-one years of data from Sweden found that women who got promoted doubled their chances of divorce, but only if they were in a marriage with more traditional gender roles. In fact, while a big salary endangered a woman's marriage in the seventies and eighties, it made little difference to the divorce rate among couples who married in the nineties.[25] And some men really enjoy the glory of their spouses' successes, either because it's a testament to their good judgment in women, or because it reflects well on them that they were chosen by somebody who's such a talent, or, ideally, because they see any win as a win for the team.[26]

So complicated is the love and money knot, and so stark are the changes of the last few decades, that a new breed of therapists who combine financial and marital advice has sprung up in the last five years. These counselors believe that couples can't really solve their money problems without also addressing their relationship issues. "People have all the financial information but they still can't move forward," says Edward Coambs, a family therapist and an organizer of the Financial Therapy Association's annual conference. "Part of what makes it difficult is that money is such an integral part of our life that we don't even realize the numerous ways it influences us on a deeper symbolic level." In these circles, using a spouse's money without permission is thought of as abuse or "financial intimate partner violence." One school of thought[27] even argues that money is the first subject therapists should address, because it flings open the door to what's really going on in people's interior lives and gets at the root of so many issues that bedevil relationships: family of origin, boundaries, trust, conflict, and power.

Coambs says a typical couple will come to him for help with a budgeting plan but won't have the "relational strength" to see the plan through. They need to sort out their frailties around money and each other at the same time. "Without the ability of the two of them to sit together calmly to talk about [finances], any information I provide is not going to be helpful," he says. "Where there are profound areas of shame, or anger or fear that can come paired with a money memory, then it's easier to get provoked in a conversation and for the person who's doing the provoking to not really understand why the subject is so provocative." It's pointless to work on the accounting without also working on the accountability.

HOW TO DIVIDE UP THE SPOILS

So, is there a particular way to handle your finances that works best? I asked more than 150 couples from around the English-speaking world to let me know how they divided up their income and expenses, and I got dozens of permutations of three answers. Some people liked joint accounts. They pool all their income and pay for everything together. "Open-door policy," said one Canadian husband. "Sunshine is good for the soul." For many this was about simplifying the bookkeeping as much as anything. "I can't fathom how you would do it otherwise," says a professor and mom of two from Brooklyn, New York. One Australian woman said her husband hates personal finance so much, he simply trusts his wife with everything. "He wouldn't even know how much is in the account," she told me. Then there's the American wife who said she and her husband had completely joint accounts. But her husband then gently pointed out that actually she had a savings account that he, the bigger earner, didn't have access to. "It makes her happy," he said. "I don't know why."

The difficulties with the one big pot of income are obvious: how to determine who gets to take a taste every now and then and how to deal with a partner who has a different opinion of how much is appropriate to ladle out for personal consumption. A New Jersey couple handle this by having separate amounts that each partner can spend built into the budget "so we don't have to be concerned about it." They do a financial check-in each week. Those less on top of things kept it much looser, saying they just let each other know if they're going to spend over a certain amount, usually about $150 to $200.

There were other couples, fewer in number, who preferred to keep all accounts separate and to divide up the expenses. "I pay one set of bills," said one wife, who married a little later in life, "and he pays a different set." This appeared to be a more popular choice among those without kids than among those with families, probably because the massive income suck that kids represent makes it too unwieldy to have separate accounts. Some people suggest that keeping individual accounts means the couple is less committed to the long term and don't really trust each other, but that's not necessarily true; they have to be very committed and trusting to believe that each other is paying his or her share of the bills. Splitting expenses down the middle isn't always fair if one spouse is earning a lot less, so the better remunerated spouse needs to be generous with the deposits. "We just don't even worry about it," one New York City lawyer in a long-term relationship wrote to me. "Anyone pays for anything and if one of us (me) gets low on cash, the other one of us (him) gives the first one (me) an infusion."

A third option, and one recommended by many financial managers, who tend to be risk averse, is a kind of yours, mine, and ours approach. A large percentage of each paycheck is deposited into a joint account to pay for household expenses and a smaller percentage goes to each partner's separate accounts, to do with as they please. As long as those percentages are agreed upon and observed, nobody gets to criticize the other's choices, even if they seem dumb. I buy my clothes at the secondhand store, but I like to go monthly and donate a lot of stuff back again. My husband will buy a crazy expensive Helmut Lang overcoat without even blinking. And then will wear it every cold day for ten years and look sharp as a No. 2 pencil, until I accidentally give it to the Salvation Army. (Wrong bag, was supposed to go to the dry cleaner.) (See forgiveness: chapter 2.) But if he wanted to spend his portion of our liquid assets on rainbow stickers, I wouldn't have the right to criticize, as long as all the family needs were met.

For many couples, a little financial independence is actually the more romantic option. "With one account, giving gifts to the spouse feels somewhat diminished," said one American architect, who runs a business with her husband. "It's just more sacrificial and generous to buy a gift with money that was set aside for you. It also maintains the mystery of how much has been spent."

Then there are folks, especially those whose spouses ran their own businesses, who preferred the three-way system because they wanted a clear demarcation of what were household expenses and what were business expenses. Mary's husband, Paul, who's an educator, wrote an award-winning book about the American West. It took him forty years. "I did initially resent Paul wanting to spend money on what I thought was a 'hobby' of historical research, so I asked him to fund it himself," she tells me. "He agreed, since our money was tight in our early marriage. Since then, anything he wanted that was only for him (his gym and trainer costs, purchase of musical instruments or historical research) he has paid for."

Most people think the third option is the fairest, according to a 2017 study[28] out of the University of Maryland, which asked a nationally representative sample of Americans how a married couple should organize their finances. Interestingly, they all felt that women who made more money should be allowed to keep more money, while men in the same position shouldn't. Gender roles haven't completely disappeared, after all.

Therapists also like the three-way system because it mirrors what a healthy marriage would look like. "It actually reflects the fundamental nature of commitment when commitment is healthy," says marital researcher Scott Stanley. "There's an 'us' and there's a 'me and you.' And 'you' don't have to disappear for the 'us' to exist."

Of course, there are some obvious steps that every couple can take. Both the frugal and the spendthrift benefit from automating their savings. Just have the bank transfer a certain amount every month to your retirement/college/ savings account. Put it where it cannot be touched. This has the added advantage of soothing those for whom finances are a source of panic. My dad, for example, figured out, when my mother went back to school and became a teacher, that the teachers' pension fund at that time was a particularly sweet deal. So they funneled nearly all of her paycheck into her retirement. She was working for almost nothing, she complained. But the prospect of it took so much pressure off my dad that he relaxed around her splurges. They have now lived comfortably on the pension (and the faint vestiges of her inheritance) for three decades. Automated savings are the Universe's gift to the free-spending, the disorganized, and the impulsive as well as those who love them.

On the other hand, budgeting, another common piece of financial advice, may not necessarily be the silver bullet to end all marital financial woes, therapists say. "I think there are some couples that really need and benefit from a very tightly scripted budget," says Stanley. "I don't think most couples, especially if they have means, need it. It's really an expression of personality." Papp, from the Couples Lab, agrees. "It's much more complicated than just, 'What's your budget?' because there are so many other ways that money can come up in their relationship discussions." For example, money arguments can overlap with family issues, such as around birthdays. "People can have very different ideas about that: from 'Why did you spend that much money?!' to 'Why did we not get my mother a birthday gift?'" says Papp. "I don't think there are too many couples where a budget would solve everything."

THE OTHER D-WORD: DEBT

One of the thorniest issues is debt, especially debt incurred before marriage. Debt is like the smell you leave in the bathroom; nobody wants to talk about it, it's embarrassing, hard to ignore, and really stinks up the joint. "It is a silent killer, chipping away at your self-confidence," writes Kathleen Gurney, psychologist and author of *Your Money Personality*. A higher percentage of people in a recent survey of five hundred divorced adults[29] found out about their ex-partner's student loan debt after they got divorced than knew about it before they were married. Debt is another one of those marital bogeymen that has loomed larger in recent years: in 1997, household consumer credit in the United States was $1.34 trillion. Within a decade, it had grown to $2.61 trillion, and by the end of 2017, it was about $3.8 trillion. A lot of that is college debt—millennials are sometimes called "Generation Debt" because of the burden of student loans—but $789 billion of it was credit card debt, which is like the nasty weeping facial sore of debt, the stuff you have to clear up immediately. So if you've managed to rack up a few unpaid bills in the last decade or two, you are not alone. It's not entirely your fault, either: in the past thirteen years median household income has grown by 4.4 percent while the cost of living has gone up almost 30 percent. Wages are not going as far as they used to.[30]

But if talking about money is like walking on eggshells, talking about debt is like walking on improvised explosive devices wrapped in barbed wire. Many people avoid it at all costs, literally. You may claim that your debt is yours to contend with and that you will take care of it eventually, but that's not really the way debt works. If you can't pay, eventually your spouse will have to, unless you die or divorce. "If you're planning to go the distance together and you land on retirement day, for example, and then one of you finds out the other has got $200,000 in credit card debt, unless you're planning to break up right at that moment, that's going to kind of affect both of you," says

Stanley. If your spouse gets into difficulties and his or her creditors require liquidation of an asset, it could be your car or possessions that get handed over, too. The prospect of all this can sure get one's dander up. So the debtor gets defensive, the partner gets panicky, and oops, that's three days of sleeping in different rooms.

Studies have shown that changes in debt lead to recently married couples spending less time together and arguing more.[31] Not only does interest compound, conflict does. Couples become more negative as financial stress grinds on and that in turn lowers the quality and connection in the relationship. Longitudinal studies have shown that the more a couple disagrees about money, the more heated and negative the arguments get.[32]

Debt needn't be the end of a marriage, however. Because it triggers such emotions as shame and guilt in the debtor and fear and anxiety in the person who might also end up having to pay, the only way forward is going full frontal, being radically transparent. Owning up to a debt and facing it together can actually be really good for a couple. One study[33] suggests that shared financial horizons and a common fiscal goal, such as paying off a debt or saving for a vacation, can bring partners closer and lessen not just financial anxiety but relationship anxiety. It's like you two united against the creditors. According to Gurney, the *Your Money Personality* author, "as couples experience success paying down debt, they start to see themselves and their partners differently and the arguing ends."

Setting fiscal goals can also have the added bonus that you learn a lot about your partner and how you differ. *Money* magazine, which frequently surveys couples about their attitudes on wealth and spending, suggests partners start to get their arms around the issue by each answering a set of questions.

- What are the three most important money lessons you learned growing up?

- What are your three biggest money worries?

- What are your three biggest goals?

- What are the three most important ways you want to use money to leave a legacy?

Financial advisers stress that you don't have to agree about the answers, but understanding what's important to your spouse will help you compromise and move forward.

I don't want to underplay how much easier it is to stay married if you're not completely broke. You can have more childcare and a cleaner and meal services and another car besides the minivan and a home with two actual bedrooms. You don't have to work as hard, or worry as much, or deal with the stress of unpaid bills or eviction or living with your parents or without heat, or in an area with high crime or bad schools.

But even if you don't have all you want or need, here's a key point to remember when hitting play on a recurring fight about your bank account: there's quite a lot of evidence that marriage enriches people, literally. It's not just the fact that wealthy people are more likely to get hitched, although that's true. It's also not just the fact that there are a lot of rent, insurance, tax, and utilities savings, which is also true. It's not even that couples who retire as couples are richer than couples who don't, although that, too, is usually true. There's a whole other psychological thing at play. For example: happily married men are more responsible, less aggressive, less likely to do something illegal, and more mentally healthy than single ones, so they're more likely to be earning. This has been documented not just in a bunch of research but chronicled in masterpieces as vaunted as *Jane Eyre* and *Failure to Launch*.

Studies using identical twins have demonstrated that married guys are more hardworking and less given to partying all night than the brothers from whom they are otherwise indistinguishable.[34] A review of almost sixty studies on the subject found that married men earn between 9 percent and 13 percent more than do single men with similar education and job histories.[35]

Data gathered from the U.S. National Longitudinal

Survey of Youth, which tracks people in their twenties, thirties, and early forties, showed that the individuals they followed who were married got 77 percent richer over time than the single folks they tracked.[36] And a 2002 study of older adults found that those who had been married to the same person throughout their adulthood were noticeably better off financially than those who had not. Both men and women who had divorced and not remarried had an average of 73 percent less in the bank than those who had muddled on through.[37] Some of this, of course, is due to the fact that married people have more support around them. They have two sets of in-laws. They have more access to government and other services, such as healthcare. One recent study attributed wage growth among married men almost entirely to the fact that men with better salary prospects were more likely to get married.[38] But it's also true that marriage is the ultimate buddy system. When financial troubles hit one of you, there's another soul with a different set of resources to help you through. And you can nudge each other to make the smart moves.

So, divorcing over money troubles may be a little like draining the bath in order to prevent the water from cooling down—you're probably going to be colder in the end. This is especially true if you're a woman, and double triple especially true if you're a woman who stayed home to raise the kids. Divorced women are much more likely to be living in poverty than married women. Heck, divorced women over sixty-five are more likely to be living in poverty than *widows*.[39] Even when marital property is split down the middle and child support and alimony are added, the spouse who hasn't been working, who is usually still the wife, will always be drawing down on what she owns, while the spouse with the experience, contacts, and job history, usually the husband, can go on to earn more.

One of marriage's many roles is a business partnership. There is an Us, Inc. You and your spouse are in a bunch of financial deals together. You comanage your kids. You may also comanage a small property, your home. You're chefs, Uber drivers, entertainment directors, travel agents, and educational consultants. If your family is anything like mine, one poor soul is Head of Cat Litter Disposal, Emergency Stain Removal, and Tedious Form Signing.

In a successful business, partners let each other know what's going on. They pitch in, they trust each other and are supportive. Transparency is key. In a successful marriage, there's one crucial other ingredient: vulnerability. Intimacy is almost impossible without it. So, in fact, I didn't hold out for very long before I told my husband about the forgone $70,000—although I emphasized that really, everyone said it was more like $40,000. He laughed, but in a really nice way.

CHAPTER 4

Family

One of the things my husband and I both like to do is ride bikes. We don't necessarily like to do it together, however. He has a very light and delicate vintage racing bike. I have a robust, stable, all-terrain clunker with a basket. He races; I commute. Nevertheless, one late summer day we embarked on our first bike date: a kid-free picnic-cycling adventure to a local park he needed to see for work. The plan was to tool around together, eat a light lunch, and then explore the sculpture and art installations in this park, which is located on an island off the southern tip of Manhattan. He particularly wanted to look at some curb details. (See *architect*, previous chapters.)

Upon finishing the eating part, which was rather hurried, I found I'd locked both our bikes safely together with my unbreakable New York City bike lock and lost the key. No more riding. Just walking. And looking at curbs, as well as for a tiny little key. After what seemed to me a *lot* of that, we had to wheel our bikes back to the ferry to get home to Manhattan. Wheeling a bike alone is hard enough; it's hard to judge where to position yourself so the pedals don't hit you in the legs. Wheeling two together, joined tightly at the crossbars, is a nightmare. We had to walk on either side of this cumbersome contraption, taking little baby steps, and stopping frequently to reset the pedals so they didn't get entangled in the other bike's wheels. Each bike had to be held at an awkward hypotenuse away from our arms but toward our feet, our speed had to match the other person's, and we had to contend with hordes of other people streaming on and off the island. Then we had to maneuver the mess of steel and wheels and gears and jutting-out pedals on and off the New York City subway, which required traversing many flights of stairs.

It occurred to me later—after I'd got home and had a nice rest—that the whole exercise felt a lot like parenting: laborious, fun-destroying, requiring high levels of collaboration and extreme dedication to not blaming the other person when things went off the rails, and often resulting in painful blows to the shins.

Many of the fights we dealt with in chapter 2—and

likely the most passionate—are going to be kid-related. Children are wonderful creatures, but they do make it infinitely more complicated to be married; all preparenting marital negotiations seem so simple in comparison, it will feel in retrospect not that different from dating. Raising a family is the most exasperating, most draining, most expensive, most difficult thing most people will ever attempt. And, unlike many domestic duties, it's getting harder.

The birth of a child has for centuries been almost universally considered the happiest day of a parent's life. This is a weird tradition, since for most women that day will bring the highest amount of pain they will ever endure and for most men the most intimate experience of another human's bodily gunk. (British popstar Robbie Williams described his daughter's delivery as like "watching my favorite pub burn down.") But if all goes well, new parents believe, the loss of dignity and of fluids will be worth it. The couple may have endured nine months of pregnancy and a day or so of agony, but they have a baby! They're a family! They made it! What people fail to realize as they break out the cigars and madly text their loved ones is that the birth was just the approach. The hard part of having kids hasn't started yet. After all, it's not walking the plank that kills you; it's the attempt to swim to shore.

Yes, children are the source of much joy, the likes of which cannot be found elsewhere. I'm going to assume

you know this. It's the prevailing theory. Having and raising younglings connects us to our ancestors and all living
creatures and every other parent on the planet. It's profoundly rich and satisfying. Given my life over again, I
would probably have more children. They are a blessing
of immeasurable proportions and teach us lessons about
love and selflessness and sacrifice and what really has
value. Plus, they're insanely cute. But this is a book about
marriage, and I feel duty bound to warn you that children
are the gift that comes with a kite factory's worth of
strings attached, many of which can tangle up your relationship with your partner. To me, the old idea of having
children to save the marriage sounds a lot like setting your
boat on fire so it doesn't sink.

Marriages often hit bumpy roads, studies[1] show, soon
after the first kid arrives. But almost nobody needed a researcher to tell them that, since couples will notice they
fight more after they have kids than they did before. (Especially those who hadn't learned how to disagree construc-
tively beforehand.[2]) It's not hard to see why. What was a
two-way street between you and your lover must now become a roundabout. Such expansion is rarely achieved
without major jackhammering. For many husbands, especially those who continue to work outside the home, this
is what the first months of parenthood look like. Your
wife, who formerly adored you, is now tired, grumpy, and

dealing with sore and occupied boobs. She's expecting you to do all the work you were doing before, as well as look after her and spend your evenings decontaminating the toxic waste zone in your child's onesie. She lies awake at night worrying about the baby, even if she just checked on the baby. She can no longer discuss the day's news, but can give you a forty-five-minute download on the possibility that he smiled intentionally.

For many women, this is what the first months look like. You went from being a human with full control of your time and body to somebody you don't recognize, somebody who leaks fluids, somebody whose emotions are weirdly muddled, somebody with a whole new universe of random anxieties and fears. You're getting inches of sleep when you need yards. Your body makes milk even if you don't want it to, and your kid wants to be fed on a schedule that seems to make no sense. Any skill you had mastered before having a baby—your spreadsheet fluency, your perfect baking, your command of the archaeology of Tunisia—is now pretty much useless. Were you formerly a highly regarded marketing executive with a portfolio of award-winning campaigns? Your baby does not care. He just wants to expel some gas.

If a couple is trying attachment parenting, the popular immersive baby-led style of nurturing that emphasizes physical contact with the child, the adjustment can feel even more head-snapping. Babies are in the bed, on the body, on the breast as much as possible. Many husbands begin to feel like a vestigial limb or a phantom: they're there, but nobody sees them.

Our kids were born about four years apart shortly before Christmas. This is kind of a drag for the kid, gift-wise, but great for us. For the first year or two we gave them their baby shower or birthday presents rewrapped; they loved the paper more than anything anyway. My husband, instead of giving me for Christmas some useful mothering item, gave me a ring. Each ring had our child's name stamped on it and their birthday. It was a reminder that he saw me as somebody besides a mother, somebody worthy of impractical stuff, like adornment. It was kind of genius, even though he got our son's birthday wrong. He's not much of a reader of studies, but it turns out that intuitively he knew, or lucked into, what research has shown,[3] which is that new mothers are particularly sensitive to their partners' behaviors and if husbands can attend to the relationship while the mother attends to the infant, then couples can negotiate the transition to parenting a little more smoothly. Men have to make up, in a way, for the temporary reduction of emotional resources brought to the marriage by women.

AFTER THE HARD PART,
THE REALLY HARD PART

Of course, adjusting to a baby is just the run-up to the much more difficult incline ahead. How do you manage all that has to be done for the next decade and a half? How do you divide up the tasks equally? The figures continue to show that while more men than ever are doing more work than ever to raise the kids—three times as much as their fathers did[4]—women are still the primary nurturers, laborers, and organizers. Let's be realistic here; some of this is a biological nonnegotiable. Her blood has been pumped through the baby's heart. The food she has eaten has sustained the baby. Any quarter inch the infant grows is a quarter inch more that her body has to accommodate. There is no gender equality in the delivery of a child: the woman does about 90 percent of the work.* And after that it's her body that produces the kid's nourishment; if she's around, the kid has all of his or her needs met. This is a time when nature has dictated that the sexes specialize.

Attachment theory, the prevailing explanation for the way humans develop emotionally, holds that infants will

---

* Not a scientifically accurate number. Margin of error ±10 percent.

attach to a primary caregiver for safety and reassurance. If there is no reliable caregiver—if the child's needs for comforting and protection are consistently unmet in those very tender first three years—his or her emotional development is going to be very warped. (In the future, for example, it will be very hard for that adult to form the kind of bonds that lead to marriage.) Usually to begin with, the attachment figure is the mom, since she's the one doing the feeding. But that doesn't mean the dad has nothing to do. Infants can have a hierarchy of attachments and they can change. And there are plenty of kid-related tasks that could be divided up equally. So far, they just aren't. U.S. Bureau of Labor Statistics figures are clear; women are still doing more. They're especially doing more of the boring parts. On an average day in 2015, says the Bureau of Labor Statistics, "women spent more than twice as much time preparing food and drink and doing interior cleaning, and over three times as much time doing laundry as did men." Slightly more than one in five men do some household chore every day, whereas one in two women do.[5] Eventually, especially if they return to the workforce full-time, as more than half of moms[6] do, this disparity is going to rankle. Even in dual-income households women do almost twice as much housework and childcare as men.[7]

One of the main reasons that couples with children

fight so much about who does what is that prior to begetting descendants, they were unaware of what a massive drag parenting is. Having kids is sold to us as this rewarding enterprise in which we make certain sacrifices but are more than recompensed with a series of unutterable joys, often involving flying a kite or teaching a kid a profound truth. Before the kids arrive, we poor fools play out the scenarios in our minds: we will go to that secret fishing hole with them and skip rocks on a lake and run away from the waves. We will introduce them to really cool music and read them *The House at Pooh Corner*/*Oh, the Places You'll Go!*/*Possum Magic*/[*your favorite children's classic here*] and spend hours just losing ourselves in crafts. And those things do happen. I will never forget the scary joy that surged through me at the look my daughter gave me after she mixed red and white paint for the first time. I'm pretty sure Neil Armstrong's awe at walking on the moon was nothing compared to how my three-year-old felt upon figuring out that you could make pink.

But those moments take up probably about 2.7 percent of the time spent in parenting small children.* The other 97.3 percent is filled with drudgery: transport, organization, reading a stupid book with no narrative arc, running cars along a track, mixing juice, filling out forms, putting

* Another estimate, arrived at by assessing what the time actually felt like.

one block on top of another, cleaning sippy cups, dressing and undressing dolls, playing an endless repetitive narrative-free game of pretend, filling out forms, filling up baths, emptying baths, cleaning poop out of baths, cooking something bland, holding a spoon in front of a tightly closed mouth because two foods touched, cleaning up the craft the kid attempted for about two minutes, rocking the kid in your arms when you're just desperate to get some sleep, rocking the kid in your arms while walking, rocking the kid in your arms while walking on sharp plastic toys. If I could get back only the time I spent combing nits out of my kids' hair, I could have written this book already.

People capable of complex thought and skilled work can begin to wonder if this is really all their life is now. The research is pretty clear that children do not make married couples happier. One scholar went so far as to note that "most cross-sectional and longitudinal evidence suggests . . . that people are better off without having children."[8] The research[9] is also clear that mothers report being more unhappy with their marriages than fathers when they become parents. Partly that's because dads get to *do* stuff with kids, while moms tend to *be* there for kids,[10] which translates to being places where epiphanies are unlikely to happen, like the changing table, or the bedroom when they're tired and cranky but will not be put to bed. They're also more likely, if they're not working, to be looking after the kids while trying to get other stuff done, whereas Dad can just plonk down at the end of a working day and bask in the childish giggles. And then there's the unequal dignity deficit. I once saw a businesswoman on the Amtrak Acela Express between Washington and New York stop planning a presentation with a colleague to give a full ten-minute detailed analytical performance review over Skype to a toddler who had done number two on the potty for the first time. Dads would not be getting that call.

When I returned to full-time employment, I put a sign on my office door, MILKING IN PROGRESS, to head off walk-ins, and I sat at my desk with my company-provided pump and expressed little bottles of milk, which I would then put in the office freezer. (Some colleagues were a bit grossed out by the milk but the young male writer in the office next door said he found the pumping sound very soothing.) My company let me take time off if there was a kid crisis and had an emergency childcare center onsite in case of a scheduling snafu. On one occasion, after I had been summoned to my boss's office for him to shout at me, I got a call from school that my child was in the nurse's office. I called my boss back and he told me to go to school. He never did get around to shouting at me. Many, many workplaces are not that kid friendly, but white-collar corporate America, as it turned out, was not so treacherous to navigate as a new parent at the turn of the millennium. My home was another story.

My husband did, I'm sure, 300 percent more than his father did as a hands-on dad. He certainly did 300 percent more than my dad did. But that still added up to not nearly enough. At one point, we had to have a little talk, in which I pointed out that we worked the same hours in paid employment. We did roughly the same around the home: he cooked, I cleaned up, he made coffee, I made the bed. He designed the home, I made sure the bills were paid. So why couldn't he do more parenting? Why were childcare tasks considered "helping mom out" and not "holding up my end of this unwieldy couch?" Pro tip: if you want to have a discussion of this nature, please read the chapter on fights first. Then it will go better than mine did. One (male) therapist advises mothers to use their "affectionate though immoveable" voice.[11]

Gender norms are sturdy as hell, it seems. Research shows that the traditional view of mothers as the primary parent is still very widely held.[12] Corporate childcare policies are still mostly crafted with the mother in mind. Dads are still the parents of last resort, who step up in a crisis, but otherwise are not what marketing people would call "children-facing"—they're just not exposed to them as much.

This is not necessarily men being lazy. They are expected to focus on earning. More Americans endorse the family structure in which the mother works outside the home only part-time than any other model; a mere 16 percent think it's best for the family if moms work full-time.[13] But for many couples having one adult work only a little is simply not a reality. According to the U.S. Department of Agriculture, which adds up the cost of housing, food, transportation, healthcare, clothing, childcare/education, and what it calls "Miscellaneous Expenses," kids born in 2015 are going to cost middle-class parents an average of $233,610 before their eighteenth birthday.[14] Please note: just up until the end of high school. Not including college.

If both parents are working outside the home, that means childcare. I'm a big fan of childcare. It is the best money you will spend. Many studies have looked at the effect of working parents on kids and the prevailing conclusion is that, especially after the first year, there is no significant difference in the kids who go to quality daycare and the kids whose moms stayed home.[15] But even if one parent does stay home or works part-time while the kids are at school, some childcare will help. This kind of supplemental care doesn't have to be fancy or cost a lot, from a teenager who plays with the kids while a parent makes dinner to a weekly cleaning lady, to a community center where your kids get to spend all day doing what they love best, playing with other kids. An interesting thing about paying for childcare: it gives parenting a monetary value. All humans, but especially, say, men who work outside the home, appreciate work more when they understand that it has a worth that you can put a dollar figure on. Try to think of your childcare expenses as an investment in your marriage and career rather than "cash we could save if one of us stayed home." A Harvard Business School study found that people who spent money to buy themselves some time (by outsourcing some of their household or childcare chores, for example) were much happier as a result.[16] Money doesn't solve all problems, but it can mean you get a human amount of sleep.

If I had to do it again, I might do my level best to get my spouse to spend a month at home after I went back to work. A new eleven-country study[17] out of the UK suggests that the most foolproof and seamless way to get the household labor divided up fairly is for men to take significant amounts of time off to be with their offspring in the very early days of the kid's life—in other words, to take paternity leave seriously. Once they've been home with the kids for a while and familiarized themselves with the routine, they are much more likely to share duties after returning to work. "When dad spends weeks/months in solo care of young children his long-term relationship with the children is closer," the study reports. "It tips him from being a helper at home into a man who relishes his competence as a parent and takes responsibility for housework and care of the home." Want to know why those Scandinavian dads are so evolved? They are offered paternity leave under very specific circumstances: it has to be taken on a use-it-or-lose-it basis within the first two years. It cannot be exchanged for maternity leave, so only dad can use the opportunity. It is well enough remunerated to be a realistic thing to do for three months. Nordic fathers have so much incentive to stay home.

The only response to that arrangement from most American families, however, is a wry laugh. The United States does not require any companies to give their employees paid time off to have children. And while some companies, particularly in Silicon Valley or in the knowledge industries like media and banking, have very generous policies, U.S. employers do not routinely provide paid family leave for fathers. In 2018, according to the Society for Human Resource Management, just 29 percent of employers offered paid paternity leave.[18] But even when they offered, men hardly took it. After shared parental leave became an option in the UK in 2015, only about 2 percent of dads took advantage of it. Japan offers dads up to a year leave at almost 60 percent of their pay, but fewer than 2 percent of men take it.

NOT ALL PARENTING STYLES
ARE CONSIDERED EQUAL

We can't blame the disparity on household chores entirely
on the culture or family leave policies, however. Part of the
problem in my house, of course, was me. It's easy to get
very invested in your way of doing things. It was clear that
I got a bigger thrill out of raising the kids, and that doing
it well, or at least not horribly, was more important to me
than to the contributor of the other half of their genes. If
research is to be believed, I'm not alone; mothers have
higher childcare standards than fathers.[19] There was also,
if I'm being totally honest, a tiny surge of satisfaction in
being the parent the kids would turn to when they needed
nurturing. To be very loved by very small beings is like
parental nicotine. You just want more of it, even if you
have to steal it from your partner.

But my way wasn't the only way to do things. Did it
matter if our son spent some time slumped over asleep in
his jumping device, like a discarded marionette, because
my husband was taking a business call? Did it matter if
our daughter had McDonald's? At four p.m.? Meaning
she wouldn't want any dinner at five but would be cranky
when it came time to sleep? In the long game, it did not.
At the time, however, it felt like an outrage.

Children are pretty tough to kill, it turns out. If your spouse is not endangering a young life, let them parent the way they parent, without criticism. For a start, they'll learn more. One time my husband brought our daughter out in insufficiently warm clothes. I said nothing, but after she began to visibly shiver he gave her his sweater and was cold for the remainder of our fun day out. (Sucka.) Another time he insisted, against my protestations, that it would be fine to leave our two sleeping kids (three and seven) while we popped in to see friends in the same building. We stayed a few minutes longer than we intended and when we got home, our son, with our daughter clinging to his waist for dear life, was talking on the phone. To 911. Saying he didn't know where his parents were. I let my spouse talk that one through with the emergency dispatcher.

Another reason to dial down the criticism of your spouse's parental habits is that yours are unlikely to be perfect, either. That's the great thing about having two parents; they each make different mistakes. When my husband was looking after our son, he fell off the bed. When I was looking after our son, he fell out of the stroller. Who's to say which is the superior parenting fail, really? You can make up for the gaps in each other.

Yes, there are some parenting tasks women do better; generally they're to do with nurturing and listening. And there are some tasks men generally do better, which are usually in letting the kids take risks and building up their confidence.[20] This is not to say that kids with same-sex parents are missing out, since the differences between each gender are less important than the interaction and partnership within the couple. Besides which, the majority of tasks could be done by any sentient being.

As your kids get older, it's so handy to have a wingman/ stunt double/hostage negotiator who can do the tasks you're having trouble with. My teenage daughter found my interest in her social activities way too intense and built a border wall around her life. But she usually let her father know where the entry points were. Parents say they don't have favorite children and I think that's true. But they definitely go through periods where a particular child is more vexing to one or the other of them. At those times, it's great for both parent and child to have someone who loves you both to do the negotiating.

Sociologists and parenting advisers say that the most effective parents are those who are "authoritative." This means they're neither uninvolved nor too involved in their children's lives. It means they're neither too permissive nor too autocratic. Authoritative parents do not run democracies, but they're not dictators. They give kids exactly the amount of freedom they can handle. They are supportive and encouraging without being claustrophobic. Think Atticus Finch, Marge Simpson, *Friday Night Lights*' Tami Taylor, Harry Potter's Molly Weasley. I do not need to tell you that this style requires the most work, both of the thinking and talking-it-through-with-your-spouse type and of the actually-being-there-and-getting-your-hands-dirty type. It's going to use all of your available bandwidth. Super-involved parenting is the most exhausting, but authoritative parenting is the most difficult. It's like threading a needle with a live worm, or blindfolded yoga.

YOU'RE NOT IMAGINING IT, PARENTING IS HARDER NOW

My mother likes to say that her kids raised themselves. I have three brothers and much of our childhood was spent terrorizing each other; in the pool, in the backyard, in the playroom, in the car. We played sports badly and music worse. Homework got done eventually unless she called us all to watch something funny on TV with her. When asked how we were doing, my parents would tell people we were "FAQ: Fair Average Quality"—an archaic term customarily used in the selling and buying of produce. FAQ was adequate for your neighborhood grocer, not good enough for your fine-dining restaurant. They've stopped saying that now, less because they've changed their assessment and more because FAQ has come to mean something else.

Her laissez-faire style is not popular anymore. For reasons both good and not so good, parents have become much more rigorous. Parent is no longer a thing you happen to be, it's a thing you do. It's almost as if children are curated these days, rather than raised. The pendulum has swung all the way from regarding kids as produce to regarding them as uncut gemstones that need to be ground and polished with pinpoint accuracy.

You can't blame parents for this; it's because the stakes are much higher. College educations are now regarded as so critical to a kid's success and financial stability, and so expensive to attain, that preparation for them starts incredibly early. If you haven't been advised by third grade that your kids need amazing grades and a fistful of extracurricular achievements to get into a good U.S. college, then you've either been homeschooling or not paying attention.

But it's not just college. Raising kids has generally become a fear-driven enterprise. There are bogeymen everywhere, from the neglectful or vengeful nanny, to the bully at school, to the teenager who's dying to sell your kid drugs, to the perv who's going to upload your daughter's sleepover pictures onto a creepsite on the Internet, to perfectly regular adolescents who turn into cruel jerks on social media. Playgrounds are danger zones. Pools are danger zones. Trampolines are danger zones. I mean, of course they are, but nowadays it seems like that's their primary quality.

More prevalent still is the nagging anxiety that you are just not keeping up; you are not taking the precise set of steps required to ensure your child's success. You are annihilating any chance that your child will be happy because you have neglected to do certain basic tasks. These fears of inadequacy start early. Are you harming your kid if you let him cry it out when he has trouble sleeping? Are you damaging your daughter by letting her co-sleep? Is it okay to give them pacifiers? Nonorganic cheese sticks? Full-fat yogurt? How much screen time is too much? What if you can't get them into that one perfect top tier preschool/middle school/high school/college/cheerleading squad?

This would all be pressure enough for people who are also trying to hold down jobs and keep a marriage together, but there's the Internet making it so much worse. I mean better, too, because you can find like-minded souls and answers to such awkward questions as "What should I do if my son keeps sticking his penis in toys?" and "How should I deal with a daughter who won't let me go to the bathroom alone?" but wow, of all the -hoods, parenthood is the judgiest. And social media tends to amplify this. In 2016, a three-year-old boy somehow managed to squeeze between the bars of an enclosure at the Cincinnati Zoo, where he was grabbed by Harambe, a four-hundred-pound male gorilla, whom zookeepers were then forced to shoot and kill. It's a tragic incident that, as any parent of a squirmy three-year-old boy will tell you, could pretty much happen to any very active and curious child. But the hatred directed toward the boy's mother on the Internet was remarkable. "It seems that some gorillas make better parents than some people," wrote famous person Ricky Gervais on Twitter. Another famous person, D. L. Hughley, added, "If you leave your kid in a car you go to jail, if you let your kid fall into a Gorilla Enclosure u should too!" More than three hundred thousand people signed an online petition requesting that the child's home environment be investigated for "parental negligence that may result in serious bodily harm or even death."

The lesson here for parents is clear: any mistakes, even if they're as minor as turning your attention from one child to another for a minute or two, may cause hundreds of thousands of people, including some famous ones, to shame you in public. A University of Michigan study from 2017[21] found that 61 percent of moms reported having been criticized for their parenting choices.

Parents respond to these higher stakes by doubling down. We parent harder. We do more, get more involved in our kids' lives, sacrifice more of ourselves and our time. We read books that explain not just that it's poor form to spank our kids but that it's poor form to give them a time-out, and even, according to one recent manual, to use the phrase "good job."[22] It seems, as the pressure to raise kids in a certain way has increased, the range of behavioral tools at parents' disposal has diminished. (To be clear, I'm not a fan of spanking. The studies suggest it does more harm than good. I just think there's a world of difference between giving your kid an enraged thrashing at every infraction and losing it once after your child has done something particularly egregious and/or dangerous for the fifth time. Parents are human, too.)

This is why the parenting years can be so difficult for couples. They are never going to agree on which of these anxieties are reasonable and which are just bonkers. It's unlikely they'll have exactly the same priorities for what their kids should focus on and, more often than not, they will have differing levels of permissiveness and discipline. Moreover, the increased time that parents spend with their offspring often comes at the cost of time spent with a spouse. That means less time for sane discussion and less opportunity to do things that remind each other that you are in the same posse, and more occasions on which opinions are aired under deadline conditions.

Because families are little ecosystems, when one child gets in trouble, it throws the whole operation out of whack. A mental illness, an arrest, an accident, or an eating disorder isn't just something that happened to one child. It affects the way parents relate to each other, it affects the way parents respond to the other children in the family and the way those kids respond to each other. It can completely absorb one parent's attention and totally take them away from the rest of the family. And if the parents disagree on how to handle the crisis, that can make the whole situation even more fraught.

But even in less dramatic times, fights over who needs to deal with the kids are like carsickness: common, requiring urgent attention, and not easily resolved. Let's say you're on deadline at work for a project that was due yesterday but got delayed because a child needed something for school. Your spouse meanwhile has a long shift, after which he or she has to do the soccer car pool run. Then you get a call from the school to say the non-soccer-playing kid has pinkeye and has to be picked up immediately and can't come back to school for two days without a doctor's note. Whose job is it to stop what they are doing, pick up the child, take the child to the doctor, fill the prescription, and organize care for the following day? Is it the person in nearest proximity or the person who is doing less for the family? Is it the person who didn't do it last time or the person whose work commitments are most easily postponed? This is an endless negotiation.

It would all be so much simpler if children would simply play along and do the reasonable and logical things they were asked to do in a workable timeframe. Unfortunately, obedience is not endemic to the human species, especially its young. Their talents lie more in the doing-stuff-I'm-not-supposed-to field. This means parents are often going to end up in a good cop/bad cop scenario. Some parents take some infractions more seriously than others. And children are notoriously good at figuring out which is which and playing the two against each other. This is tough, because you're not always sure in advance what issues the two of you are going to feel differently about. Nobody ever sits down before they get married and says, "When we have teenagers I expect them to be in by eleven p.m., to have only as much pocket money as they have years on the planet, and to wear no outfits that display side boob until they are eighteen. Thoughts?" It's beyond our powers of abstract thought to imagine the disciplinary techniques we might need to use on children we don't have for infractions they have not yet committed. We aren't even necessarily aware of what our parental lines in the sand are, since they are more or less imbibed from our parents and rarely articulated.

I remember well the first day I said the F-word to my mother. She said nothing, but I tossed and turned until my shroud of guilt just about choked me, then apologized. I failed to pass such qualms along to my kids, who talk to me like they're card-carrying members of the Crips doing a long stretch at juvie and I am the puniest warden. At first, I objected, but my spouse did not, and the kids sensed the fissure and played it up. After many attempts to curb

the bad language—including charts, a curse jar, gentle re-
minders, the removal of privileges, the withdrawal of certain toys or digital devices, a reward for going a week
without swearing, a complicated trading system involving
one person refraining from offering advice if another re-
frained from swearing—I just gave up and did my best to
ignore it. Which also, for the record, didn't work. Without
my spouse's help, it was impossible to hold back the influence of all the music, movies, and neighborhood behavior
my twenty-first-century New York City kids experienced.
It probably would have been impossible with him. At
some point you and your spouse need to have a conversation about which disciplinary hills you wish to die on, and
then suit up to defend those. You might still lose, but at
least you'll go down together.

WHEN YOU HAVE TO TAKE SIDES

It's tempting, especially when things aren't going so well
with your spouse, to default to siding with your kids. And
it's easy; we're almost biologically programmed to do it.
They are so easy to love, especially when they're little and
susceptible to the magic of a hug. But we choose to love
our spouses. And we have to keep choosing to do so. It's a
different kind of love and not just because it involves sex.
Loving your kids is like going to school—you don't really

have a choice. Loving your spouse is like going to college—it's up to you to show up. But it's a bad idea to prioritize the kids over the spouse. First of all, kids turn into teenagers and want very little to do with either of you. Then they leave. They don't want to be the object of all your affection. After about twelve or thirteen years on the planet, they will greet any public display of warmth with revulsion, suspicion, or sullenness. Relying on your kids to be your companions and helpmeets is like relying on junkies to look after your valuables. They just can't. They have other priorities. And it's unfair of you to ask them.

Second, studies strongly suggest that kids whose parents love each other are much happier and more secure.[23] They have a model of not just what a relationship looks like but of how people should treat each other. This is actually what the old saying "charity begins at home" means. People learn how to be charitable to each other from the behavior they see in their families. (This was a shock to me, as I grew up thinking this meant that our parents should give money to us instead of donating to a needy cause.) In his bestselling book, *The Meaning of Marriage*, Tim Keller notes that the privileging of children over spouses all the time hurts families. "If you love your kids more than your spouse," he writes, "your entire family will be pulled out of joint and everyone will suffer. And I do mean everyone."[24] And yet when the writer Ayelet

Waldman proclaimed in an essay[25] that while she loved her four kids, she was in love only with her husband, it caused a public scandal.

Keller is a pastor and might be seen to be biased toward marriage, and Waldman is an essayist who might be seen to be biased toward hyperbole, but actually a bunch of research tends to suggest they're right. Kids are deeply affected by their parents' relationship. Diary studies (when parents keep a diary of the days' activities at the end of each day) have shown that mishandled tensions between a couple tend to spill over into parents' interactions with their kids, especially among fathers.[26] Other research has found that children whose parents are often hostile to each other blame themselves for the fighting and do worse at school.[27] A 2014 survey of forty thousand UK households revealed that adolescents were happiest overall when their mothers were happy with their relationships with their husbands.[28] One of the best things you can do for your kids is love the heck out of your spouse.

Both sociologists, who examine the issue from twenty thousand feet in the air, and therapists, who have a microscope over people's lives, find evidence that kids from what are known as intact marriages, as a whole, do better on most fronts than kids from divorced families, unless the marriage is very high-conflict. (Of course, I will keep repeating, just in case people don't read every chapter, some marriages are just too toxic to sustain, and if a spouse or child is in danger, he or she must leave and take the kids.)

This issue is very tricky and highly regarded scholars have come to different conclusions from studying the data. Obviously, lots of children from couples who separated are perfectly fine. But the stats are not encouraging. Research[29] suggests that in the long term, children of divorced parents are more at risk of behavioral, psychological, health, and academic problems, and of being poor and getting divorced themselves. These effects may last well into adulthood and the negative effects even if the divorce takes place when children are grown.[30] In fact, psychologist Judith Wallerstein argues that the cumulative impact of divorce increases over time.[31] It's true that the financial hit that follows many marital splits might be the cause of many of the other adversities, but studies that have taken income into account still found that kids from bifurcated families face more challenges than those from parents who stayed married.[32] The takeaway from this is not that nobody should get divorced; it's that children benefit when marriages are good, so it's counterproductive to favor them at the expense of a spouse.

Often parents get so invested in the enterprise of parenting, of getting it just right, that it moves from an activity they were undertaking as a team to the point of the team's existence. In fact, some modern scholars have ar-

gued that parenting is really the only reason people get
married anymore: it's the most efficient and reliable way
to successfully manage the labor-intensive long-term enterprise of having kids.[33] Then after the kids have moved
out, they're not quite sure what to do. It would be like
asking the members of Real Madrid soccer team to keep
traveling together but just not play the games. There's no
point. Lacking a common purpose, they split.

This is what therapists say is behind some of the recent
rise in so-called "empty nest divorce" or "gray divorce."
Gerontologist Karl Pillemer of Cornell University, who interviewed seven hundred couples for his book on what
makes love last, says one of his biggest discoveries was
how dangerous "the middle-aged blur" of kids and activities and work was to people's relationships. "It was amazing how few of them could remember a time they had
spent alone with their partner. It was what they'd given
up," he says about his research. "Over and over and over
again people come back to consciousness at fifty or fifty-
five, and can't go to a restaurant and have a conversation."

The only way to inoculate yourself against this outcome is to remember that—scholars be damned—the kids
are not the reason you got together; they're a very absorbing project you have undertaken with each other, like a
three-dimensional mobile jigsaw puzzle that talks back
and leaves its underwear in the bathroom. One mother I
interviewed for this book described the kind of teamwork

she needed as a parent as "one of us robbing the bank and the other driving the getaway car." Sometimes this kind of partnership will require taking a vacation without the kids. On other occasions it will simply require remembering to put the other adult above the kids now and then.

What does that look like? I think I might have mentioned, in passing, that my spouse is an architect. Having an architect in the family means that should you travel anywhere, you will have to see buildings. Not just wonderful churches and interesting art galleries, but public housing, local government offices, or even private homes whose owners are not that psyched about gawkers. Many of these masterpieces will be, let's say, off the beaten track. (One of my spouse's bosses made his family travel to a building in France that was so far away from where they were that by the time they got there, it was dark. So they just felt the building.) And when you get to your destination, there will be photographs. Not snaps of you and the kids (unless you give an idea of scale) but of details: how a window meets a corner, a stair tread, where the banister is joined to a wall, the guttering system. Somewhere in my husband's archive he has several dozen photos of the disabled elevator at the Louvre. He has none, however, of the *Mona Lisa*. The kids would rather do something that involved retail. I would rather do something that involved nature. But my husband gets so exhilarated by these architectural excursions, that we go. Wherever we are, we spend some time looking at buildings, because when we put it to a vote, I (nearly) always vote with my teammate. Also because families are not democracies and parents win.

And cliché as it sounds, do not underestimate the value of spending a night on the town—or anywhere there are no children really—just with your spouse. The key is to get enough uninterrupted time together to remind each other of who you are and what it is you saw in each other. Or, failing that, just check in and make sure you're not missing anything vital. "People must, not optionally, but must, carve out this regular space for couples," says Pillemer. It doesn't have to be fancy. One of the couples he interviewed just used to go to McDonald's. Esther Perel, the infidelity specialist, suggests breakfast dates. (You send the kids to school and take a "personal day" from work.) Most people will be a couple for many more years than they will be parents. You don't want to lose those doubles skills; they'll come in handy.

HOW TO NOT GO NUCLEAR ON
YOUR NONNUCLEAR FAMILY

Nearly all matters related to raising children—especially finding affordable childcare for the occasional nights or mornings out—are much easier to handle if you have family around to help. The problem with that is that you then

have family around. To "help." This was not our problem.
We had loving families a full day's flying away. If my spouse
and I wanted to go out, we had to pay somebody Manhattan money to look after the kids. At one stage of my career, I was more or less obliged to go to movie premieres.
(I know, the horror, please send thoughts and prayers.) For
a stretch of several years these were the only dates my husband and I did. It was either stay home and eat mac-and-
cheese or go hang at a wrap party with George Clooney
and pay off the babysitting costs with an installment plan.
Anything less enticing was not worth the outlay. On many
nights, we'd yearn for more family and talk enviously of
friends who could drop their kids off with their in-laws
and just go hang out.

But as you know, in-laws are a mixed blessing. Ernest
Hemingway's wife Martha Gellhorn said that no woman
should ever marry a man who hated his mother. I'm aware
that thousands of women, on the other hand, think that
sounds like the perfect arrangement, if it means they
won't have to see her. A middle course between the two
might be to regard your in-laws roughly the way Canada
regards the United States—as a useful and friendly ally,
but not an overlord. I have Indian friends who were among
the first in their families to wed for love, rather than by
arrangement. As if that weren't novel enough, they also
decided they didn't want to have kids. At one family gathering, the husband's mother, hoping to steer her daughter-

in-law away from this course, began to offer a little advice. Her husband bounded over from across the room and planted himself between his mother and his wife. "If you want to talk about this, you talk to *me*," he said.

Your loyalty is to your spouse before your parents. This can be tough, especially if you're still quite fond of your parents, as I am, and feel vaguely guilty about times you may not have been a model offspring, as I nearly always do. When my parents visited—and this is very Australian—they tended to stay with us in our one-bathroom apartment. While I loved having them, I would often be quite exercised by my mother's opinions of my husband's and my life choices. Then my brother whispered to me the most solid gold little nugget of advice: "You need to turn down your mother-receiver," he said. "You're picking up way too much signal." Sometimes, it's more loving to mindfully ignore the opinions of the people who saw you through those first years of life and kind of forgot that you grew up.

Do whatever you can to try to stay on good terms with your in-laws, if only for your kids' sake. Grandparents—and uncles and aunts—can give them a really solid sense that they come from somewhere. Research on resilience has shown that a large number of high-quality relationships helps kids bounce back from adversity. And while studies on grandparents are quite rare, some research suggests that kids who have a close relationship with their elders are less likely to be depressed as young adults.[34] This intergenerational harmony, or its rough equivalent, will be easier if you assume that everyone's intentions are good and you decide that the primary objective of any visit to your in-laws is to remind them what an agreeable person you are. (The works of Jane Austen offer amazing research on this.) You may actually find, as I did, that your children open up a previously unexplored avenue for connection with your parents and your in-laws. You both have a vital interest in this new little being, and it's a subject you can discuss that has no history, at least at first. Of course, they're going to have opinions on childrearing that differ from yours, but they are just that—opinions. They're not orders. There's no harm in the R & D approach (Recognize and Disregard). Your parents-in-law are largely responsible for creating your life partner, so you owe them at least one favor per visit. If grandpa and grandma are truly horrible and toxic, and the kids are going to see nothing but fighting, then take a pass. Research suggests parents' relationship with grandparents is the key factor in how much influence they have and whether it's a good one.[35] For the record, my in-laws are lovely.

The writer Jamie Malanowski lost his brother to a viral infection when he was seven and his brother was fifteen. After that, he kind of lost his father as well, as the man buried himself in his work to blunt the force of the grief. "He took the second job. He increased his over-time," Malanowski wrote in an essay for *Time* magazine for Father's Day. "And when he was around, he more or-bited his family than functioned as a part of its nucleus. Often when he tried to fit in, it was awkward. It took an effort. By the time I was a teenager, I wasn't much inter-ested in trying." But after he had his kids, a different man emerged. Already seventy, he really played with Malan-owski's daughters. He would pretend to be hurt and let them bandage him. He went on roller coasters with them, took them to petting zoos. "Along the way, something un-expected happened: He and I grew closer," Malanowski writes. "Part of it, I'm sure, was that I was more mature, and that since I had become a father, I more clearly ap-preciated all that he and my mother had done for me and my siblings. And what they had lost. But part of it, too, was that he had changed." Malanowski's experience, while extreme, is played out among families everywhere. Don't let the opportunity of getting to know your in-laws or parents in a different way pass you by.

Sometimes it feels like parenting is custom-designed to suck all the joy out of being with your partner. But it's not; it's just a huge adventure that is much better faced together. The abortive bike picnic date isn't my family's worst bicycle story. That would be the night some poor idiot tried to steal the vintage racing bike from the corridor outside our apartment. He was interrupted by my spouse who, wearing only his undergarments and Ugg boots, chased him through New York City streets at three a.m. The perpetrator, who was on said bike, got clean away, but then circled back around (it seems calculating risk was not his long suit) and my husband took after him again, this time shouting "Bike thief!" The enraged bellowing—and I'm guessing the idiosyncratic outfit—alerted the cops, who had been called by neighbors and were driving past, as to the thief's whereabouts. They caught up with him three blocks away. The next day we discovered my husband had broken his toe. Soon after that, we got the bike back.

This is an allegory for parenting while married, in which the felonious individual is your children and the bike is your relationship. In the heat of the moment, with all the effort you're expending and all the dignity you're losing in the pursuit, it will often seem like the love you had for your spouse has gotten away from you. But with persistence and a little help—plus some shouting and broken bones—you can get it back.

CHAPTER 5

Fooling Around

The other night my husband couldn't sleep. He's a spectacularly gifted sleeper—middle seat of the plane, uneven ground on a campsite, mid-conversation about the kids—he can achieve full REM slumber under almost any conditions. So I knew something was up. And I knew he had a big day ahead at work. "Anything I can do?" I groggily asked, mostly to be polite. He suggested we have sex. It was three a.m. I wasn't really awake. I was not in the mood. Unlike him, I find sex tends to wake me up. But the opportunities to do your spouse a solid without even getting out of bed do not come along every day. Moreover, humans who have not slept are not as fun to be married to as those who have. So we went at it, and I noted with some satisfaction that not long afterward, he dozed right off. (To clarify, I mean after, not during, the sex. Thanks.)

I understand that this is not a sex scene that romance novelists are going to steal for their next book. Nobody working in the porn business is dog-earing this page and reaching for their highlighter pens right now. That particular episode was the kind of affectionate, easygoing, sloppy entanglement that two people who have loved each other a long time can enjoy, but it's not the kind of sex we admire— the kind we put in movies or describe in songs or aspire to as a culture. I bring it up not (just) to show off my mad bedroom skills but because of what it says about the sex life of couples who've been together a long time. We make love for a variety of different reasons, including desire. That reality is both beautiful and terrifying, because it collides with everything we have been raised to believe about sex.

Making love to your spouse is that rare thing: something you can do for no money with no guilt nor strings attached in under an hour in your own home without polluting the atmosphere or oppressing the downtrodden or getting fat, that can nevertheless be body-shakingly mindblowing. That such an activity even exists is astonishing. It's an extraordinary gift from nature. There is no experience during which I've felt more exhilaratingly out of control than having sex with my husband. And yet, despite all the fun it offers, sex is one of the chief sources of pain, estrangement, and bewilderment within couples. The marriage bed can so easily become a slab of despair, self-loathing, and bitterness.

Take "Kelly," for example.* A fifty-ish working mom from Missouri, Kelly says she has not attempted to have sex with her husband of twenty years since 2015. After being married for thirteen or fourteen years, she says, her husband simply lost interest. He had trouble getting aroused, and Cialis only worked spottily. Finally, after one rejection that involved him swatting away her hand in bed, something broke in her. "I had an overwhelming flood of feeling deeply alienated and deeply abandoned," she says. "I tried really hard not to let him know and instead went to the bathroom and started sobbing into a bath towel." When the kids leave the home, Kelly expects they will divorce. In the meantime they're taking lovers on the side, so it's clearly not just about his physical function. "Neither of us is willing to throw our kids to the wolves just because their parents can't get their sex lives together."

In no other activity are our bodies and our emotions so inextricably entwined as they are in making love. Well, maybe skydiving, but no activity that most of us engage in with any regularity. And yet, while we understand, for example, that not every meal we prepare for our family is

---

* For the record, "Kelly" is a real person with kids and parents. This is her version of the story. For obvious reasons, I did not check it with her spouse. Her request for anonymity seemed entirely reasonable to me.

going to be an incredible feast, we often arrive at marriage expecting every sexual episode for the rest of our existence to be effortlessly transcendent. And if it's not, our emotions can go into a tailspin. Hardly anybody leaves his or her spouse for someone whose cooking is more exciting. But people leave their partners for a different bedmate all the time. People even leave, or cheat on, spouses whom they love, and love being married to, just for the boudoir novelty. Sex has that terrifying power.

THE CRISIS OF DESIRE

Bedroom satisfaction is one of the primary ways by which most people, like Kelly, measure the health of their marriage.[1] Yet many many couples aren't getting it on as much as they'd like. A "sexless marriage" is the term for a union in which making love does not feature strongly: some sources say that means people get it on fewer than ten times a year and others define it as less than once a year. Given people's proclivity to not tell the truth about their intimate activities, it's unlikely the surveys are very accurate, but they estimate that between 2 percent and 10 percent of all marriages are sexless. According to one American accounting, about 25 percent of married couples believed their marriages were sexless within two years of the wedding, when they're still allegedly in the easy part.[2] Perhaps more tellingly, lack of sex is the most common marital problem people talk to their computers about. In 2015, there were sixteen times more searches on Google about a spouse not wanting sex than about a spouse not wanting to talk.[3]

You'd think, in this era of effective birth control and Viagra and the increasing acceptance of a wider variety of sexual unions and acts, that couples would be having more sex than ever. But a 2017 study[4] found that sex is on the wane all over the United States. Using data from the General Social Survey (GSS) conducted by NORC at the University of Chicago, which has asked thousands of people about their sex lives since 1989, researcher Jean Twenge calculated that in 2010–2014 the average American had sex about nine fewer times a year than the average American of 1995–1999. According to even more recent figures, which GSS director Tom Smith calculated for me, the number of people getting it on at least once a week fell from 45 percent in 2000 to 36.2 percent in 2016. And married couples had the steepest drop over this period—51.8 percent had at least weekly sex in 2000 but only 37.5 percent in 2016.[5] (However, in a rare show of unity on this subject, all studies find that on average, married and cohabiting people have more sex than unmarried people. This shocks most married people I know and almost no single people.)

What is going on? Why do people not wish to have sex

with the people who are right there in bed beside them, who are theoretically willing, whom they love and whose sexual druthers they are very likely to know? Psychologist Esther Perel has been studying "mating in captivity," as she calls it in her 2007 bestseller of the same name, for years. She traveled to twenty countries to talk to people about desire and found that wherever people got married for love, there was "a crisis of desire." What did it stem from? The warring nature of having and wanting. What we value about marriage and committed relationships is dependability and security and proximity and the ability to be completely ourselves and yet not alone. But those things do not feel sexy. There is no erotic threat in being reliable.

Perel's work follows in the footsteps of psychoanalyst Stephen A. Mitchell, who saw many relationships collapsing because the security blanket they provided was so heavy, the couples' ardor was smothered. "In its raw form, lust is not a pretty thing," he wrote in his book *Can Love Last?*, "and is difficult to reconcile with other features of romantic love, such as respect and admiration." Bill Gates, for example, has many admirable qualities, none of which put him in any danger of ever being named *People*'s Sexiest Man Alive.

For many, however, the problem does not feel like admiration but its opposite: How do people bring themselves to feel passion for somebody they don't always like? That same spouse who hasn't shaved her legs in a week. That same spouse who makes that annoying clicking noise at the back of his throat. That same spouse who just threw you under the bus at a dinner party. How do you keep the fires going? How do you keep craving the person who is always there?

Desire, somewhat inconveniently, is most easily provoked by something we don't possess; for the new, the unknown, and in some cases, the forbidden. As anyone who has watched a teenager staring into the refrigerator for the fourth time in twenty minutes can tell you, nobody hungers for stuff that is on hand. There's a reason extramarital sex partners are often referred to as strange, used as a noun—as in, "Every time I start thinkin' on my age, or that I'm bound to die, I start thinking about *getting some strange*."[6] The word "longing" suggests you can't have it for anything that is close. Psychologists call this the "intimacy-desire paradox": we partly desire sex because we crave intimacy, but high levels of intimacy can seem to inhibit rather than enhance desire.

These days, most of us will live longer than our parents and grandparents lived. And we will be physically healthier and therefore capable of bonking for longer. Whatever reservoirs of physical attraction we had when we first got together with our spouses are going to have to hold out for quite a stretch. And we have higher expectations of our sex lives than our forebears. "This is the first time in the history of humankind where we are trying to experience sexuality in the long term, not because we want fourteen children . . . and not because it is exclusively a woman's marital duty," notes Perel.[7] "We want sex over time that is about pleasure and connection." Of course, this is a somewhat female perspective: men have been expecting a lifetime of hot sex since there was sex to be had. But their lives were shorter—and there was no Viagra.

Any activity that is repeated will inevitably lose some of its thrill, as the brain becomes accustomed to it. This is a helpful brain mechanism that allows us to build memories and learn what to expect in certain situations so that we can acquire skills to handle them. It's important to acknowledge that this is a feature of human biology, not a glitch. Madeleine Castellanos explains it well in her book, *Wanting to Want:* "At the beginning of a relationship, your brain is rewarded for paying attention to every little detail of a person, and sexual desire is enhanced by novelty and discovery. Because your brain works to be efficient, it gives less attention to the same person over time since there is little new information to be gathered in that interaction. Don't blame your brain for this, it's what helps you learn and function in the world."

Our ebbing desire also helps us to steward our energies.

(And not just humans. Male guppies, given unlimited access to a variety of female guppies, *schtup* as many as possible. However, it comes at a cost; they do not grow as large as monogamous guppies, perhaps because they're too busy guppling up to forage for food.[8]) There is not necessarily anything broken about you or your spouse's system if the craving for sex recedes over time. Novelty does not last. The sight of our spouses naked or an urgent expression of passion no longer gives us such a rush. Our reservoirs of desire go from overflowing to needing a refill.

REFUELING THE TANK

So what's a couple who love each other but don't feel physically hungry for each other all the time to do? There has been much research into what impedes libido—a Latin word Freud reintroduced because "lust" had a bad reputation—but not a lot of clear answers. "It's not even clear what desire is, let alone how the activity of different parts of the brain combine to produce it," Barry Komisaruk, a Distinguished Professor of psychology at Rutgers University, told the BBC. "No one can do that reverse engineering yet." Like the number of plastic containers you have in your cupboard, desire is going to wax and wane according to an incompletely understood set of conditions. Sometimes, you have so many old take-out holders and random Tupperware that you can hardly close the plastic container drawer. Other times, you just run out.

Ian Kerner, psychologist and author of the bestselling sex book *She Comes First,* likens desire to the stock market, responding to a myriad of influences. "There are ups and downs and it's very dynamic," he told me. "There are numerous factors that work in combination; there's almost never one issue to be solved." For each couple who ends up on his couch, he says, he has to figure out the biological, psychological, and social issues at play. "Desire," he says, "is multiply determined."

But when the plastic containers run out, it's not a bad idea to look in your fridge and see what old and stale items might be coming between you and access to your Tupperware. What do you need to toss to make room in your life for some more nookie? As Emily Nagoski, author of the bestseller *Come as You Are,* points out, sometimes it's easier to turn off the things that inhibit our sexuality than to try to continually juice up the things that excite us.

Desire, the theory goes, is a dual system: there are accelerators and there are brakes. Accelerants are any phenomena that whisper of sex: the energy of a new relationship, your lover's face or body, the excitement of reuniting with a person after they've been away, a hot breath in your ear, a beautiful sunset. The decelerators are those things that suggest sex would be a bad idea. They are legion and can be either physical or emotional or relational and very often do not rise to the level of conscious thought. In long-term monogamous relationships the accelerators start to have less power. And those brake pedals get very touchy.

So how can you loosen them up? There are several physical factors that are known to reduce sex drive. Research proves it, but you probably don't need studies to figure out what they are: excessive alcohol, weed, and a lack of exercise can put a dent in your sexual enjoyment and lower your drive. Obesity can, too. There are psychological hindrances as well: depression and horniness are almost mutually exclusive, but alas, the same is often true for taking antidepression medication. Stress can do a number on passion, as can resentment, low self-esteem, and interpersonal conflict. Fear, for both physical or emotional safety, will usually smother desire. I live in a New York City loft. The privacy is imperfect. This has sometimes proved to be a pretty effective brake.

Nagoski takes particular aim at that old bogeyman, body image. "Your body is the one and only thing you have with you every single day of your life, from birth to death," she says. "You can fight it and hate it and rage against it. And you can welcome it and love it and embrace it with compassion and kindness." So few people over the age of four enjoy the sight of their bodies—or the thought of being seen—naked. Yet David Frederick, an associate professor of psychology at Chapman University in Orange, California, who has studied body image for years, says this fear is misplaced. "Men and women overwhelmingly were satisfied with their partner's appearance," he told the *Los Angeles Times*.[9] "People are more critical of their own bodies than they are of their partners'." Fear that your equipment is nonstandard, say therapists, is also unfortunately common, even among married people. Whatever you've got, though, you're more than likely good to go. For example, the clitoris, the only organ on the human body that appears to exist solely to give its owner pleasure, has an estimated eight thousand nerve endings and can be from 0.5 to 3.5 millimeters in length. That's a sevenfold difference in size. (If you don't know where the clitoris is, put this book down, and google it. Now. You can thank me later.) I can guarantee, on the other hand, that nobody has a penis that is seven times bigger than your penis. There is no standard size or shape for genitalia, despite what porn suggests.

I have always suspected, for example, that I'm kind of a substandard lay. My husband, I felt, had married up in terms of sunshine, goofiness, and money, but beneath his station in coolness, looks, and boudoir aptitude. Thus, even twenty-five years in, I'm always a teensy bit nervous about sex, as if I'm being asked to play doubles with John McEnroe. (I keep half-expecting him to say "You cannot be serious!") And my body confidence has not increased with age and gravity. So I know how hard it is to fully embrace the truth that it is highly unlikely that you are grossing your partner out. And yet, my body is the number one attribute my husband compliments.* "When you get right down to it," Leonore Tiefer, a New York City–based sex therapist and educator told me, "the building blocks of being sexual are about comfort with nudity and being touched and smelling things and hanging out in that awkward space."

Another big, wet, suffocating fire blanket, therapists have observed, is resentment. In modern homes, that resentment is often powered by the division of labor. Believe it or not, there has been quite a lot of research into the link between desire and housework, and no small amount of academic dispute. One study[10] using data from the early 1990s found that couples in traditional gender roles—male breadwinner, female homemaker—got it on more often. The researchers suggested that when people behaved like the other gender, there was less sexual charge

---

* I once wrote an essay about the pain of being married to somebody who was widely regarded as better looking (it's an "interfacial marriage") and a few TV talk shows asked us to come on the air and talk about it. My husband declined, because, he says, the essay was pure fiction. The man is no idiot.

between them; they were too similar to attract each other. But this was countered by more recent studies[11] that found exactly the opposite—that guys who do more of an equal share of household chores get to mess up the bed more often. Those researchers suggested that as husbands and wives worked out a more equal division of labor, each grew less resentful, and marital happiness grew and led to more sexual happiness.

Interestingly, one marital researcher[12] found that among women, always having to wash the dishes had a particularly strong correlation with sexual misery. Daniel Carlson, an assistant professor of family and consumer studies at the University of Utah, speculates that it may not be the Palmolive that's peeving them. It's the perception that they're getting a raw deal. "Since 2006, dishwashing has become the least likely chore to be done only by women," he says. "If a woman looks around and sees other husbands and partners doing the dishes, and in her home she's the only one who's doing it, that affects how she perceives her situation." It's less about the work, he believes, than about whether her relationship feels fair. (By the way, the same study found that the most sexy chore was grocery shopping. Not because groceries are crazy erotic, but because it was the chore most often done together. Plus, it got people out of the house to somewhere less familiar.)

Some therapists have suggested that our work lives can be brutal on our sex lives, too, because of the stress we bring home with us. Research[13] suggests that even the expectation that people were checking emails at home was a strain on domestic happiness. For that reason, it's probably a bad idea to bring devices to bed with you (sex toys not included). Answering emails just before you go to sleep or planning the next day's meeting do not set the mood. Nor for that matter does scrolling through Facebook or Instagram. And watching different TV shows on different screens while lying next to each other is parallel play, not foreplay.

A 2018 National Bureau of Economic Research working paper[14] looked at data from four million people in eighty lower-income countries and found that TV ownership was associated with a 6 percent drop in likelihood that a couple had had sex in the previous week. And, interestingly, the decline in the sexual frequency of married couples discussed earlier in the chapter started in about 2000, just as broadband Internet was reaching most homes. "The No. 1 recommendation that every sex therapist will give is to get the technology out of the bedroom," says Canadian sex researcher (a lot of sex researchers are Canadian) Lori Brotto. "The bedroom really should just be saved for two things and two things only." When your focus in bed is on a screen, it cannot be on your partner.

And if your partner is trying to get your attention, it's disheartening to be ignored for a slab of glass and microprocessors. Dismay and horniness cancel each other out.

Of course, the emotional and physical impediments to sex are interrelated. People who are obese have worse body image. The spouses of those who drink a lot are often resentful. People under a lot of stress find it hard to get aroused. One huge example of this is sleep. A 2017 study found that older women who got less than seven or eight hours a night were also less likely to engage in sexual activity with their partners and reported less sexual satisfaction.[15] An earlier study found that women with greater average sleep duration reported "better genital arousal," which is academics' adorable way of saying they had more fun in bed when they were awake.[16]

How do you help your partner sleep better—I mean apart from the methods I outlined in the beginning of this chapter? People who talk to their spouses about their day and whose spouses respond with interest get to sleep faster and slumber more soundly. It's not hard to understand why being able to vent some built-up pressure to a sympathetic ear might help sleep, but in one experiment among military couples,[17] talking about the good stuff helped as well. This is not just about letting your partner chat on while you wonder if the car needs servicing or if it's your turn to bring the soccer snacks or if the dog always smells that bad. It's about listening. More powerful than being able to talk, the studies found, was the realization that you had been listened to. People who felt that their spouses were responsive to them slept better. Even without sleep, people—especially women—are more likely to be in the mood, studies[18] have shown, if their partners listen and respond to them, to make them feel connected.

One of the things you may want to talk about and respond to, incidentally, is sex.

THE UNIQUE AGONY OF THE SEX TALK

When we got married, my husband and I were required by the laws of the state of New South Wales, Australia, to attend premarital counseling. Unlike much of my mandatory education, this instruction turned out to be surprisingly frank. Our counselor was a church minister, who was also our friend's dad. So when he said that one of the hardest parts of being married was articulating to your spouse what you liked and needed in bed, all three of us looked off to the side at whatever object we could plausibly claim was fascinating. But he had a point. Most of the names we have for our intimate activities and body parts are also curse words or insults for drivers whose skills we don't respect. The language of intimacy is not very beautiful; it can be clinical, it can be filthy, it can be funny, but it is rarely poetic. This is why there are so many atrocious sex scenes in books. (I speak to you as a woman who was professionally obliged to read *Fifty Shades of Grey.* Twice.)

Nevertheless, sex researchers have discovered that those who talk about having sex more have more and better sex. William H. Masters and Virginia E. Johnson, who did for sex research what Ben and Jerry did for small-batch ice cream, were insistent about this even in the sixties. Throughout their pioneering book *Human Sexual Response*—the result of monitoring more than ten thousand sexual encounters in their Saint Louis, Missouri, laboratory—they extol the virtues of straight shooting to partners about what excites them. They bemoaned their subjects' "persistent neglect" of open communication and "potentially self-destructive lack of intellectual curiosity about the partner."[19]

They also noticed that in terms of orgasms, the homosexual couples they observed were more efficient than the heterosexual couples. That's kind of a well, duh, discovery, since people are usually much better at knowing how to work equipment when they have that same equipment back home. So the gay guys, they observed, were more aggressive in their actions with each other, because that's what men liked and the lesbians were gentler and slower

with each other, because that's what women liked. But—
and Mary Roach puts this well in her terrific history of
scientific studies on sex, appealingly called *Bonk*—"the
other hugely important difference Masters and Johnson
found between the heterosexual and homosexual couples
was that the gay couples talked far more easily, often, and
openly about what they did and didn't enjoy."[20]

Yes, things have changed since the sixties, but not that
much. A 2012 study[21] quizzed almost three hundred married individuals from the Midwest about how much sexually frank talk they used and also about their marital
satisfaction and closeness. The results showed that people
who used more sexual terms, especially slang terms, were
closer and more satisfied. And interestingly, the results
were particularly strong for women. Because it's not clear
of the direction here does the frank talk cause the happiness or the happiness allow the frank talk?—there was a
follow-up in 2014 in the *Journal of Sex and Marital Therapy*, which asked 293 already happy spouses about their
sexual disclosure habits. And sure enough, respondents
said that talking to partners about what they liked in bed
led to greater relationship satisfaction and closeness. Also,
interestingly, most of the stuff spouses said to each other
was encouraging and instructive.[22] Again, should we really need studies[23] that show people who talk to each other
about sex have better sex? No, but just like those signs in

restaurant bathrooms about washing your hands when
you're done, the obvious sometimes needs to be spelled
out.

The rector who met with me and my husband-to-be
was right; discussing sex with your spouse is not as easy as
it sounds. For example, when is one supposed to have that
conversation? Not while the kids are around, I'm guessing. Not mid-act, lest you ruin the mood. Not at the shops.
"Do you want to get Colgate or Crest? Speaking of which,
do you like it when I nibble your nipples? Oh, and do we
need butter?"

Even if we can find a suitable private moment, a lot of
us get squeamish and struggle to find a way to say anything at all. Lonnie Barbach, the highly respected clinical
psychologist and author of *For Yourself: The Fulfillment
of Female Sexuality,* has said that the most important sentence in the English language is "A quarter of an inch to
the right, please," but that's a much easier instruction to
give in a relationship in which sex is a familiar subject,
which it very often is not. "There's a vast amount of lying
when it comes to communicating about sex," says Leonore Tiefer. "People are ashamed and they're afraid that
they're bad and broken and defective because of the culture and the time we live in. Everybody takes it personally:
'I'm too fat and I don't know what I'm doing, and am I
really supposed to think that?'"

Kerner, the New York City sex therapist, likes to get

the couples he counsels around this squeamishness by having them describe in detail their last sexual episode. "If a couple has made it in here, they don't get a choice whether they talk about sex," he says. "I ask them a lot of questions to enable them to describe their last sexual event like a slow-motion replay—from where it happened, when it happened, how it was initiated, how desire was expressed, how arousal was built, and the activities they engaged in." The full postgame analysis, he says, is really helpful to him for two reasons: it's very diagnostic, in that he gets to see the dynamics at play. And it breaks the sexual ice. "I'm asking them to use a language that is sexual and intimate. Part of the power of talking about sex—it's not like talking about money or real estate—is that the language itself can be physiologically arousing. I want to get them comfortable with the poetry of sex and the language of sex."

One way to get used to the "poetry and language of sex" without wading into the weeds of postgame analysis is to simply ask your spouse to describe a sexual fantasy. If he or she could do anything or have anything done, what would it be? This doesn't necessarily have to be something that you then rush out and do. It's just a non-threatening way for your partner and you to get a look inside each other's head and get used to talking about sex. "Just share some really resonant sexual erotic thematic material, from your unique sexual personality," suggests

Kerner. "I think that is honestly the key towards being in a long-term relationship and being able to reap the benefits and yet still bring something that is unique and quirky and taboo and kinky and unpredictable and novel."

The theme here seems to be vulnerability. It takes courage to let your spouse see your murky inner workings and subterranean thoughts. You want to be admired and your fantasies may not feel particularly noble. "Sometimes in hookups I think what's exciting is people just say, 'What the heck, this is what I want, do this to me.' Because they don't care, there's nothing to lose," says another sex therapist, Laurie Watson, who hosts a weekly podcast called *Foreplay*. "But with their partner they worry if they say, 'Hey, do this to me,' their partner is going to call them a pervert or denigrate them for having this fantasy or idea. There's more at stake because we're connected, we're going to be with that person in the morning."

WHO WANTS WHAT WHEN

Men want sex, by and large, more than women do. This is not news. While some researchers suggest that there may actually be more variation within genders than between them, XXs and XYs certainly come at the issue from different on-ramps. The data is pretty strong on this; various studies have shown what we anecdotally already know: men will pay for sex, women almost never will.[24] When a relationship is developing, guys want sex before women do.[25] Men think about sex more often than women do.[26] Men's attitude to casual sex is much more relaxed than women's is.[27] Male same-sex couples have more sex than female same-sex couples.[28]

For men, sex is primarily a physical thing; for women, it's a way to connect. Evolutionary biologists might explain it this way: women seek connection because they are born with a limited number of eggs and they need to make sure the ones that get fertilized can survive, for which they need a third party to commit to and invest in them. Whereas guys make new sperm all the time, so they just want to off-load as often as possible; the more seeds you plant, the higher the likelihood of getting a tree. Neurologists, on the other hand, might point out that during orgasm, men's brains do not release quite as much oxytocin, the so-called "bonding chemical," as women's brains release, so sex remains a bodily rather than a relational experience.[29] Their brains are more influenced by dopamine, the chemical connected with the anticipation of thrills. And therapists might break it down the way Laurie Watson did for me: "For her, sex is a byproduct of the warmth of the relationship, whereas for him sex is the heating element. It's what warms him up, it's what makes him feel connected and loved. She needs to be talked to and feel close before she has sex, and he needs to have sex in order to feel vulnerable and willing to open up."

So. This is going to cause some tension, no? Let's add to these discrepancies the facts that women's libido plummets for a while when they have kids. And then slowly declines further after menopause.[30] Men's sex drive remains more robust, and while they might not spring into action quite as crisply after forty, they have medication to keep them solid into their declining years.

Result, in the broadest possible strokes: Men want more sex. Women want more intimacy. Throughout history, couples have made various accommodations to their partnership to manage this desire discrepancy, as it's known, or were forced into them: concubines, mistresses, open marriages, polyamory, or other versions of what modern thinkers refer to as the side ho. But none of those has really caught on. Most couples do not survive an affair. Open marriages are still, by and large, a curiosity.

Of course, you can have a desire discrepancy with your partner no matter your gender. "I never crave sex," wrote "Hazel McClay" in a recent anthology about women.[31] "So if I never had it again, I don't think I'd miss it. If I never had another brownie, now, that would bum me out." On the other end is "Renee,"* who told me she

* A real person, who told me her story on the condition I used one of her middle names because she has kids.

dressed differently, talked differently, wore a bustier, promised to not wear a bustier again, got out of sales into a less stressful job, went to therapy, took her husband to therapy, and offered him all manner of sex acts, in an attempt to get him to have sex with her more often. "He felt very strongly that women felt sex was a need," she says, "and in his opinion, it wasn't." They divorced.

One helpful aid for navigating a libido imbalance might be understanding the difference between spontaneous and responsive desire.[32] I like to explain this difference with my dad's favorite joke: A church decides to have a season of abstinence. Nobody is allowed to make love for a month. One day, as the congregation gathers to tell their stories, a newlywed husband confesses that he slipped up. "My wife was bending over to pick up a can of paint and I just took her right there and then," he says. "Well," the pastor replies, "you are no longer welcome at this church." To which the husband says, "Yeah, we're no longer welcome at the hardware store, either."

Those hardware store urges, the prompts that just appear amid the cans of Intense Teal and Bluebird Feather, are spontaneous desire. Those are the ones we always see in movies, read about in romance novels, or hear about in songs. There's a clear sequence of events in those encounters. Desire, followed by arousal, followed by orgasm. There is another path, however; some cravings take shape only once you start painting, when you weren't sure you liked the color until you got it on the walls, and then you realized how amazing it looks. That's responsive desire; it arrives after the party has started. Canadian (yep) researcher Rosemary Basson codified this model after noticing that up to 30 percent of women thought their sexual appetites were abnormally low. "Rather than concluding that some one-third of women have a 'disorder,'" she wrote, "the reasons for this apparently common perception of failing to meet some sexual standard must be sought."[33]

Sexual desire doesn't have to be linear. Basson suggested it might be better represented by overlapping circles. A woman, for example, may decide to make love to her spouse for any number of reasons—procreation, affection, boredom or, ahem, maybe even to help him sleep. (Texan college students came up with 237 distinct reasons that they or their friends had had sex.[34]) At many points after the conscious decision is made, she can begin to feel the tinkling of the desire keys, even *after* the arousal. Humans can experience both sexual cycles, but usually, men are more spontaneously desirous, while women are more the responsive types.

For people to feel desire, what their genitals are feeling and what their brains are feeling usually need to be in alignment. So if their genitals are feeling stimulated but their brains are elsewhere, sex simply may not be that exciting a prospect. Indeed, it may be very unwelcome. And if their brains are ready and willing, that doesn't mean their genitals will automatically juice themselves up. Nagoski has put it this way: "Your genital behavior just doesn't necessarily predict your subjective experience of liking and wanting."

A spontaneous desirer, whom for the purposes of this explanation we shall call Spondo, might say, as a couple gets ready for the day, "Do you want to have sex tonight?" And a responsive desirer—let's go with Respo—might not, as he or she tries to find keys and phone and worries about traffic, feel particularly lustful. That does not mean that Respo isn't going to have sex that night. It does not mean that Spondo is unattractive. It just means Spondo cannot expect Respo to feel as he or she does at that moment. "We're so narcissistic in our bodies," says Watson. "We believe that our body tells us the absolute truth. And what my body tells me I believe your body is telling you." Of course, both men and women want to feel desired. But not all desire arrives at the same time. People with Respos for partners often feel unloved; they want to be wanted. But when Respos need a little space to clear their minds and focus on their sexual system, that doesn't mean they're not in love; their system just runs on a different timetable.

Both Spondo and Respo have contributions to make to

a happy sex life. Respo needs to understand that he or she is actually the one calling the shots—Spondo's engine is always humming; Respo is in charge of getting the vehicle to move. He or she has control of the parking brake and gearshift, and lust may not always be the most optimal way to decide when to engage them. Wanting to do something is not the same as being willing to do it and see what happens. Respos have permission to start to get it on without waiting around for lust to appear, if they want to. That doesn't make sex fraudulent.

For their part, Spondos can help create an atmosphere with as few sexual inhibitors as possible. Is the house a teetering mess? Are the kids all accounted for? Is there a privacy issue? Is their partner feeling loved and desired or is he or she feeling more like the easiest route to your climax? One thing Spondos should not do is force, guilt, beg, or otherwise coerce their partners into having sex. That's a desire annihilator. "Lasting sexual desire comes when your experiences around sex lead you to want to have more sex," writes Castellanos.

Sex within a committed relationship is often like taking a walk. I know this sounds deeply unerotic, but bear with me. Sometimes, it's a gorgeous spring day and the trees are just budding and you're in the hills of Vermont or Sussex or Victoria and you just can't wait to be outdoors to take it in. And then, just as you walk up the gently undulating slope, the sun comes out from behind the clouds and you see the first daffodils and the birds begin to sing and you come to a clearing and for several seconds right in front of you there are bear cubs frolicking or a lyrebird singing and showing off its tail and holy crap it's totally breathtaking. You see stuff you've never seen before. And then the fauna withdraws and you walk back down the hill, deeply content.

Then there are those walks that are just ambles around the local park that you took to get out of the house. Maybe a kid kicks a ball. Maybe you see a dog. All the same, hardly anyone comes back from a walk wishing they hadn't gone. The only wrong kind of walk is the forced march, the one you do on threat of punishment.

For those of you too pressed for time to go for a leisurely stroll, even a brief, purposeful walk has benefits. Studies have shown that testosterone is produced by cuddling, as well as by sex. In fact, Sari van Anders, a professor of psychology and gender studies at Queen's University, Ontario, (which is in Canada) tested women before and after they had cuddled with partners[35] and found that they had a greater increase in testosterone than after they'd had sex. "Our study appears to be the first to report that healthy women with higher T [that's science speak for testosterone] report more orgasms; these findings lead to the possibility that increased T from sexual activity might lead to increases in sexual desire or orgasmic experience," she writes.[36] Cuddling, unlike coitus, is a completely acceptable public activity, so you can do it anywhere, even—or especially—in front of the kids. If you want to feel more sexy, keep touching your spouse. Use any excuse to get your skin on his or hers. Massage, a morning cuddle, sleeping naked, a hand on the knee during a drive, whenever you feel it might be welcome.

The science and the therapy line up here, since many therapists suggest exercises designed to help couples just keep touching each other, not necessarily sexually, but in playful and tender ways. "Desire comes from the interaction—physical and emotional interaction between the two of them . . . it's this combination of anticipation and touch,"[37] Barry McCarthy, a psychology professor at the American University in Washington, D.C., told *The Washington Post*. McCarthy, along with Michael Metz, a psychologist, marital therapist, and ex-Catholic priest (a trifecta!), developed a model of what enduring desire might look like—the Good Enough Sex model—that, despite its comically unambitious name, has become highly respected.[38]

McCarthy's model emphasizes moving away from a performance-oriented, everyone-wins-a-coconut-every-time attitude toward sex to a mutually assured intimacy, in which couples work as a team to overcome the physical and psychological challenges of keeping desire alive. It's a combination of realism and using what you have—which means a lot of gentle touching. With work, sometimes quite a lot of work, says McCarthy "the majority of couples who are motivated can rebuild sexual desire." You can become each other's erotic allies, pushing back whatever forces— kids, in-laws, age, fear of making an embarrassing noise— are conspiring to come between you and nookie.

THE CORRECT AMOUNT OF SEX

Inevitably, if one member of a couple thinks they're not having enough sex and the other thinks they are having too much, there is going to be a numbers fight. Numbers give us an illusion of certainty; in math, there's usually a right answer. So everybody wants to know: How much sex should we be having? Therapist and author Marty Klein hates this, because it can make a problem of what is not a problem. "People come to my office and say to me, 'Tell me how often people have sex,' and I won't do that," he says. If you and your partner are happy with the number of naked encounters you have, just go forth and bonk.

But if it helps to screw down (sorry) a number, then some Canadian (*again*) researchers were brave enough to pick one: once a week. According to a 2016 study,[39] couples having sex more than once a week do not report being any happier than those who have, say, a regular Thursday night assignation. Couples who have it less than once a week, however, report being less happy.

That study cast a big net. It was based on an analysis of the results of surveys of more than thirty thousand Americans collected over forty years in three different cohorts. But I urge you, before looking up from this and glaring at your spouse, be aware that any study of happiness is always really about correlation and not causation. It's possible that people in happy relationships have sex once a week, rather than vice versa. It's also possible that people are content having sex once a week because they think that's what their neighbors are having. It's *more* than possible that people are lying to survey collectors about their sex lives.

Therapists acknowledge that it can seem bogus and lame and mannered to have a specific night set aside for sex. But when things get hectic or kids sap your energy, being spontaneous may simply be outside the realm of possibility. "What else do you do in your life that's of value to you that's not planned?" asks Lori Brotto. "Really, nothing. When you plan sex and you talk about it, it opens up possibilities to fantasy and anticipation, and actually thinking about the factors that give rise to a pleasurable sexual encounter." Having a little flag fluttering there in your mental calendar can reduce the tension around whether sex is ever going to happen again. It can also diminish the fear of rejection or confusion. If that night becomes impossible, the two of you can at least discuss it and know why. Alternatively, some counselors also recommend a little sign that you might want sex, a pebble in a jar or a particular coffee cup at breakfast that's a secret between the two of you.

FOR WOMEN ONLY—OR THOSE
WHO MARRIED A WOMAN

Women's sexuality still perplexes most who study it—or live with it. Here are just some of the gray areas: Studies report widely different numbers on how many women need clitoral stimulation[40] to climax.[41] Half a century after it was first proposed, the existence of the female G-spot—an exquisitely erogenous zone inside the vagina—is still the subject of academic debate. So is the purpose of the orgasm. Some women who have spinal injuries that should prevent any sensation from their lower abdomen reaching their brains can feel stimulation in their vaginas[42] and orgasm. Women don't seem to have a refractory period; they can climax multiple times, one after the other.

One team of neurologists who captured images of female brains during orgasm found that many different parts were activated, including the amygdala, which is involved in social judgment and vigilance.[43] But a Dutch team using a slightly different method found that there was *less* blood flow to certain areas of the brain—including the amygdala.[44] "At the moment of orgasm, women do not have any emotional feelings," one of the study authors, Gert Holstege, memorably told a conference in 2005. And most women have what's poetically called "brain-genital disagreement," when they don't consciously feel aroused by something but their genitals are. In one study[45] women were shown videos of bonobos mating and blood flowed to their vaginas but they felt no arousal. The only female sexual desire drug to emerge so far, Addyi, has largely been a bust.

In short, women's desire is a complicated thing. "It's a dreadful disappointment to both men and women," says Laurie Watson. "Men say to me, 'Wow, I got to do all this work to arouse her and get her going.' And I say, 'Right, because you married a *woman*.'" The complexity of female sexuality does not make it inferior to males'. It's just different. And it doesn't improve anybody's sex life to make it conform to the script sold to humans from birth— the fast, hot, single-position, mutually orgasmic romp, achieved in three minutes or less. "She's looking at herself, hovering over the bed, thinking 'Oh my god, nothing's happening. It's probably not my night,'" says Watson.

Much journalism, academic thought, and pharmaceu-

tical research has been devoted to methods of kindling female desire. Lori Brotto has done some promising studies
using mindfulness with low-desire women. She trains
women to begin to focus on their bodies and shut out dis-
tractions. Her theory is that it will help in brain-body
concordance, so that women will notice what their bodies
might be responding to. "We're improving their ability to
notice internal body sensations," she says, including
changes in their skin sensitivity or breathing rate, so they
might be able to more seamlessly access their desire. "We
also find improvements in mood, reductions in stress and
distraction, and improvements in overall quality of life."

We live in a culture that sends very confusing messages
to women about sex. There's the only-sexy-women-are-
valuable message, which seems to contradict the equally
prevalent   women-who-are-sexually-aggressive-are-scary
message, which also contradicts the women-who-don't-
put-out-are-uptight-control-freaks message. In her book
The Sex Myth, Rachel Hills observes that underneath so
many of our sexual hang-ups there's a perplexing subtext,
"the belief that sex [is] more special, more significant, a
source of greater thrills and more perfect pleasure than
any other activity humans engage in." Speaking from her
own experience, she notes, "I didn't feel unattractive and
inadequate just because I was not having sex. I felt that
way because I lived in a culture that told me that my sex

life was one of the most defining qualities of who I was. It wasn't the sex that was the problem, but the importance that I and so many others had attached to it."[46]

But it's not as if men have it easy, either. They're encouraged to see sex partners as conquests and the ability to bed attractive women as a sign of superior skills, while also warned that all sex needs to be mutually agreed upon in advance. It's not yet clear what our dawning awareness of and vigilance about sexual assault will have on sex in marriage. But in a perfect world, it could cultivate more thoughtfulness about sex as a means of communication and intimacy building and expression and not just a mutually beneficial orgasm-generating activity. "We have a long way to go before people have a sense of how beautifully crafted the whole arousal potential attachment system is," says Leonore Tiefer.

This brings us to that old bugbear: porn. There are two schools of thought on porn, both of which claim to have science on their side. One is that porn is harmless and might even, as some Canadian researchers[47] found, improve your love life, if watched with your partner for suggestions, to promote discussions, and mutual arousal. The other is that porn is the opposite of harmless. The proponents of this theory suggest that watching porn conditions the brain to respond to the sexual cues sent from the screen rather than those emitted by flesh and blood.[48] They note that bedroom difficulties are reported among men of all ages who hit the porn very hard. And learning how to have sex from porn, these critics believe, is a bit like learning how to handle a gun from spaghetti westerns. (It's also possible that a third thing—some problem in the brain or the culture—is causing both the sexual dysfunction *and* the excessive porn use.)

Regardless, in the vast majority of cases, porn depicts a particular kind of sex, one that focuses on male gratification—it's all about speedy penetration and thrust, and much less about the caresses and slow build that women enjoy. In that way, it's a very poor form of sexual modeling and seems designed to arouse only one partner. (As somebody who once watched movies for a living, I also find that porn lacks narrative arc and character development. But that's probably like pointing out a stain on a bed of nails.) Many therapists I spoke to noted that since the advent of broadband Internet, porn had become a big wedge issue between couples. It's worth considering if porn's making your partner feel undesired, fearful she doesn't match up to the standards of the porn stars. She might also wonder why her lover is choosing a screen for sexual gratification over her. This could do a number on her self-esteem and sexual confidence, and, as noted before, low self-confidence can shrink-wrap desire until it's less accessible than a toy in clamshell packaging.

Given all the variables, the smartest move for a happy sex life might be to rely on that old standby: self-determination theory. The tenets of this theory suggest that we humans are most content and healthiest when we regularly indulge in activities that allow us to choose and control what we do, feel confident and capable, and draw close to other people.[49] That is, we have autonomy, competence, and relatedness. That would mean the most radiant sexual interactions would be the ones that would permit us to do the things we like, do them well, and feel loved as we do them.

The good news is that despite the fact that menopause does sap us all of libido, sex can actually be easier as you get on a bit. For one, women are usually more familiar with how their body responds, so sex becomes a more positive experience for them. Moreover men, less driven by their testosterone, can embrace what McCarthy calls "affectionate, sensual, playful, and erotic touching as a bridge to sexual desire"[50] rather than just being hell-bent on intercourse or orgasm. Over the course of many years of monogamy, a couple may naturally be less overwhelmed by the appeal of their partner or by how special they feel in their partner's eyes. But they have the opportunity to build an incredible connection. And it's almost impossible not to be thrilled if you still bring someone delight.

The equally good news is that sex and long life are

linked. Researchers Barry Komisaruk and Beverly Whipple[51] have found that people who have regular orgasms seem to have less stress and lower rates of heart disease, breast cancer, prostate cancer, and endometriosis. British epidemiologist G. Davey Smith and colleagues found that in a given decade, the risk of death among men who had two or more orgasms a week was half as great as those who had less than one a month.[52] And the most famous of all sex researchers, Alfred Kinsey, believed that sex could dull pain, and that it brought on, as Roach writes, "a biological priority shift," which led to "a sexually mediated disregard for pain and physical discomfort"[53] in which fevers and muscle pain died down. That is, she adds, "whatever ails you pretty much stops ailing you during really hot sex." Your afternoon quickie could quite literally be saving your partner's life.

Karl Pillemer, the gerontologist who interviewed more than seven hundred older adult Americans, reports that none of them said that they found their spouses unattractive. Not a single old person. And these people were really old. Partly, the gerontologist argues, we imagine that we can't keep having sex with the same person for decades, because the idea of people older than us having sex just grosses us out, in the way that accidentally walking in on our parents grosses us out. (I learned to knock after doing that just once. The image still burns.) One seventy-seven-year-old who was still having a go with his wife put it this way: "Somehow as you get older, you kind of get blind to the infirmities that affect the other party. And you always see them the way they were. You don't see aging. It's a wonderful thing. I don't know if the brain is wired for that, but that's the way it is . . . whatever you're doing, just keep doing it."[54]

—

CHAPTER 6

Finding Help

I t was my husband who suggested we visit a therapist.
Since the man hates to talk, the proposal made me sit up
a little, like a dog hearing an unfamiliar footstep. I knew
things hadn't been great, but I'd figured we just needed
to find a way to have some fun together. When I jokingly
suggested our time and money might be more profitably
spent on a date night, he just smiled wanly. The vaguely
buzzing alarm in the back of my brain kicked up a notch.
And another, when I discovered he had already found a
therapist. Sue was not the chic intellectual I'd imagined
he'd be drawn to, but a gentle hippie-ish flowy dress–
wearing woman who reminded me of his mother, Patty, a
woman whose advice he has not taken since he wore short
pants.

It transpired that my spouse had come to believe that

he was unloved, that the kids and my work were all I cared about, and that he was just another thing on my to-do list. It transpired that he felt like a roommate and was wondering if he still loved me. It transpired that the therapist was a last-ditch effort before he decided to call it quits.

These revelations provoked in me a fury of which I did not think I was capable. To me it seemed that every single part of his life had always had to and would always have to stand in line behind his first love, which was architecture, and that our whole family had arranged our lives to accommodate that passion and merely hoped to satisfy ourselves with whatever gleanings of devotion were left over. How dare he, who gave his family such desultory attention, now claim to be the unloved one? I even had at the ready, without knowing I'd amassed it, a well-developed list of the occasions on which he had put his family's needs second: the time I had mastitis and a newborn and he went out clubbing; the winter we had all been cold because he wanted to install a floor-to-ceiling window and it wasn't ready; the lack of an oven. And now *he* was threatening to leave *us*?

In other words, ours was a classic case. We were dealing with two draining jobs, young kids who needed a lot of our time, very little bandwidth for each other, and a not particularly rompish bedroom. Resentment, bitterness, stress, debt, sudden pangs for other people: we had the complete package. Almost every bad but legal thing a human can do to another human, my spouse or I had done or attempted to do to each other. The Four Horsemen of a doomed marriage—contempt, defensiveness, criticism, and stonewalling—were holding a daily parade in our living room.

To find our way out of this morass, we sought guidance from Sue for about two years, every second week. It was tough. Hearing the person who knows you best detail for a stranger the many ways in which you suck ranks between "lost at sea" and "ten miles in heels" on the fun scale. And sometimes the disclosures in that room led to worse arguments afterward. Which then had to be picked apart at the next therapy session. And so on. It felt like perhaps airing it all was making it worse, like we had been thrown into the Great Therapy Pit of Carkoon to be digested over and over again for a thousand years by the Sarlacc. At least that's how it felt to me; my husband is not so much into *Star Wars*. More of a *Blade Runner* guy. (And no, this did not get sorted out by Sue. She seemed to think we had more pressing issues.) Since we met during lunch hour, I used to bring a sandwich for each of us from my local fast casual joint, which we would eat afterward in a sad little concrete park, often in morose silence. Every time I go to Pret A Manger now, I can still taste the despair.

But eventually, some problems that used to be insurmountable were understood, recognized when they cropped up, and worked around or joked about. Wounds that had us doubled over in agony began to smart a little less as they were shared, explored, and forgiven. Sometimes, having another brain in the room can change the way you talk about a persistent problem. It helps locate the fuses, so you know to keep your lit matches away from them. A different set of eyes can detect the patterns where the mention of issue A sets off response B, which leads to retaliation C and then stonewall Z, which is a reminder of issue D, and so on into eternity, and notice a way to disrupt them. One prominent psychotherapist, Daniel Wile, likens couples counseling to being in the observation tower at the airport. You can see the feelings arriving and leaving, even if they're unscheduled, and notify the folks in the high visibility vests to make the appropriate adjustments.

My husband and I learned to talk differently about stuff when we got home. We had a lot of conversations through gritted teeth that started, "What I am hearing you say is that you don't like me touching you when we're with other people," which sounded super-mannered and fake and ponderous, but actually did get to the nub of the issue: "No. What I am trying to say is that I often wish you were as affectionate in private as you are in public." The thing about having those irritating, inauthentic conversations that therapists recommend in which you repeat back what someone is saying, is they do kind of force you to listen, and not just to lock and load while your beloved is talking.

Slowly, over the course of many months, as we began to clear a backlog of grievances, get to the source of recurring fights, and understand why we each behaved a certain way, our resentment and fear of being taken advantage of began to ebb and was supplanted by a sort of compassion. The word *cherish* became a useful one: How might I make this person feel cherished? Our therapist was a fan of the concept of love languages, the idea that we each have a primary method by which we transmit love and receive love, and they're not necessarily the same. If our partners are not speaking our love language, we may not be able to translate it. The theory is that people can show love through gifts, physical affection, loving words, acts of service, or spending time with their lover. In the same way, people believe they are loved when somebody does one of those things for them. The nice Southern pastor who came up with this idea, Gary Chapman, wrote a book, *The Five Love Languages*, that has been the bestselling marriage book for about a quarter of a century, so while there are no peer-reviewed studies[1] to support his theory, he may be onto something.

Eventually, my husband and I began to think of ourselves as a team. It wasn't totally the therapy. My job changed—I got a demotion, or promotion, or sideways-motion—and became more flexible. Our kids got a little more self-sufficient. His work situation became less precarious. He got out of a stressful business partnership. Mostly we stopped acting as if our marriage was some frictionless object that would sail along forever without any energy directed its way. We changed our relationship to our relationship. "We" became important to us again.

THE MCKINSEYS OF MARRIAGE

What do big companies do when their enterprise begins to go pear-shaped or wobbly? They call in the consultants. They pay through the nose for an objective, expert third party to take a look at the books, the assets, the debits, the work flow, the whole shebang, and to offer some advice. And they're not embarrassed about it when the people from Deloitte or McKinsey drop by. Yet married couples, with so much on the line, often don't seek outside assistance until it's too late. John Gottman[2] estimates that couples wait an average of six years too long before seeking help. Therapy is like car maintenance. Or spring cleaning. Or blowing the lint out of your laptop. Why would you not want to look after this institution that protects your health, your wealth, and the well-being of your kids?

Yet most people don't want to go to couples therapy, just like I didn't. In 2015, the Australian government of-

fered any couple who wanted it two hundred dollars'
worth of marriage therapy for free. The theory was that a
saved marriage represented thousands of saved dollars in
potential family court costs and child welfare payments.
But the elected official who championed the policy also
believed that happy families were better for society in general, and so the government could legitimately fund such
a scheme. Worried that there would be a deluge of requests, the program was capped at one hundred thousand
couples. Seven months later, only ten thousand couples
had registered and many of those had not actually gone to
counseling. The government scrapped the program and
spent the $17 million it had left elsewhere.

For similar reasons, the state of Oklahoma, which has
one of the highest divorce rates in the United States, put a
lot of resources—a reported seventy million dollars' worth
of its federal welfare funds—into marriage education programs between 2000 and 2016, with similarly tepid results.
One evaluation[3] of the program suggested that one of the
reasons for its ineffectiveness was difficulty in finding participants.

This reluctance to seek help makes complete sense.
Therapy costs money (most therapists recommend at least
twelve sessions at an average of $100 an hour, which is not
usually covered by insurance[4]), it's awkward, it uses up an
hour that could have been spent having fun. All of this
would appear to exacerbate the problems that you have

already: financial pressure, poor communication, and a lack of time for each other. Also deep down, people don't think they're broken. The relationship is probably fine. They just need to talk more/have more sex/go out more! It's a mystery why that isn't happening.

And last and extremely relevant, couples don't think it will work. They're just going to have to listen to a whole lot of mean things being said about them and then nothing will change. "I found if you have to go every week for an hour, all kinds of stuff gets said that you wouldn't ordinarily say, that you would just bury," says Gary,* who tried five different therapists but is now divorced. "So you're hearing even more negative stuff because you've got to fill the time. We walked out barely speaking." He and his wife, who had different ways of communicating and different personalities, found it difficult to find a counselor they both liked. And the need for help struck them at different times. "It's got to be rare for two people to both wake up the same morning and think, 'We need to go to therapy and we need to cover x, y and z' and be on the exact same page. I would bet in a huge percentage of cases one of them is just going to get out of the doghouse."

While there are no hard figures on this, therapists say it is still usually guys who are more reluctant to do couples therapy, partly because they don't see the problem and

---

* Not his real name but a real person.

partly because men are still less likely than women to seek assistance with any mental health issue.[5] But even if it's not the guy, often at least one partner thinks that if his or her spouse would simmer down, everything would be fine. They go to therapy as a way of appeasing their spouses, or so that the therapist can tell their partners not to get so upset at stuff.

Not every therapist disagrees with people who throw shade on their discipline. One big study[6] that checked in on 645 couples five years after they first reported being unhappy found that those who had stayed married were glad they were married. On interviewing fifty-five still married spouses in depth, however, very few of them attributed their happiness to counseling.

Part of the problem, psychotherapists say, is that couples counseling is among the most difficult of all therapy to do. Augustus Napier, author of *The Family Crucible*, who worked with one of the pioneers of family therapy Carl Whitaker for five years, has decided that it's so difficult, he prefers to do couples therapy side by side with another therapist. "The demands of this practice, of working with families and couples, are much greater than we had anticipated, and the therapists need a lot more help, a lot more structure, a lot more support in order to do it well," he told a fellow psychotherapist in an interview. "When trying to work with families and couples alone, I've often found myself triangulated in some way, or compromised by that process, or feeling overwhelmed or discouraged, or induced into the family's own world to too great of an extent."[7]

Psychotherapists don't all agree on what to counsel. Some, including bigwigs like John Gottman, think that many problems between a couple cannot be solved (if someone wants to move for a job and the other doesn't, for example) and instead people have to learn to live with the difficulties. Others, including Susan Heitler, a specialist in conflict resolution and author of *The Power of Two*, believe they can get a couple to a place where they can negotiate a solution that works for both of them on nearly every issue.

Despite all these caveats, data has shown that couples who are really distressed don't get better without therapy. This book, I hope, can help you figure out some ground rules for making a marriage more fun, but there are some types of problems for which you need to call in the professionals. After all, getting on with another human for a long time is not that natural a thing to do. Hardly any other species can manage it (mole rats, wolves, beavers, voles, gibbons, and some birds, mostly not the attractive ones). There will be problems, and some of them might be too complicated for the people inside the relationship to figure out. Very few people not called Jason Bourne can perform surgery on themselves.

Even couples who have mastered the basic skills outlined in the fighting chapter are going to find them hard to
access when the going gets really emotional. It's not unlike
driving on curved roads, where people with average skills
are fine at the normal speed limit but get in trouble if required to drive much faster. When the really important
and difficult subjects come up and people get agitated,
even really good communicators spin out of control. "You
can teach people communication skills until you're pur-
ple, and they'll even learn them if they're good clients,"
says Sue Johnson. "[But] when you really need those skills,
which is when you're in a completely threatened state and
all caught up in negative emotions with your partner, you
can't access them." Even she, a highly respected practitio-
ner who has taught therapists around the world, still fights
over stupid stuff with her husband. All her training can
do, she says, is help her to figure out how to recover the
couple equilibrium more quickly. Similarly, what therapists using Johnson's techniques do is provide a place to
rehearse the behavior couples are going to need when
things go sideways, or shortly afterward. "We don't teach
people skills. It's too artificial," she says. "We give people
new experiences." Counselors who offer her form of therapy get couples to role-play actual situations to identify
where their triggers are.

Couples therapists are also able, as neutral observers,

to probe into vulnerabilities stemming from family history, or trauma, or mental health that many spouses may be in too much agony or emotional distress to notice or reveal. And unlike individual therapists, they don't, if they're good, represent one partner or another. They're advocates for the couple, for the union. (This is not to say that individual therapy won't help a union. Most therapists believe that it's almost impossible to have a fulfilling marriage if one of the partners is too psychologically wounded.)

A good analogy for marital therapy might be physical therapy—it's right there in the name. The theory is that you can repair a weakness or injury with some changes to behavior, including building up the muscles around the problem area so they can support further healing. During treatment, a therapist observes your challenges, teaches you certain skills, has you practice them in front of him or her, and then sends you off to do a lot of reps at home. But most of us don't approach marriage therapy like that. We treat it more like the emergency room; hauling ass in there only when things have suddenly gone horribly awry, begging to be fixed.

For example, infidelity.

IT'S NOT THE SEX, IT'S THE BETRAYAL
(BUT THE SEX DOESN'T HELP)

Infidelity doesn't happen in a vacuum. It's always a symptom of a bigger problem, usually either with the cheater or with the partnership. By some estimates—and the number is pretty hard to pin down—70 percent of couples who seek marriage counseling do so because one of them has been caught cheating on the other.

Louise is one of them.* She had been married thirteen years and her daughter was eight years old when she and her husband started seeing a therapist. Her husband is British and Louise is American. They had dated while studying in the UK, then became friends when she moved back home. He came for a visit and they got married on a bit of a lark after his visa to the United States ran out. "We thought we were hilarious," she says. "Just jumping on the subway to City Hall with our $15 rings." The marriage was full of socializing and friends, but they didn't communicate well. When they argued, he'd cut her off if she raised her voice. "I'm not shouting," she'd say. "Do you want to hear shouting?" Their sex was regular but a little rote. They didn't spend much time alone with each

* All of the examples here are real people, but these are not their real names.

other. He played a lot of videogames, up to ten hours' worth a day, she says. She often felt unloved and overlooked. "It was death by a thousand cuts," she says.

She fell into an affair with a coworker. "It was like everything everyone says," says Louise, about a decade later. "It was deeply emotional—almost like dropping emotional acid." She and her colleague kept trying to break it off, but they kept coming back to each other. "At the time I thought, 'No, *this* is different. This is special,'" she says. "To my annoyance, it turned out to be the same old cliché."

Louise started going to an individual therapist, and that therapist suggested a marriage counselor. Desperate, she looked in the phone book and chose the first one she found. "There was no preinterview. It was like: You can see us? Let's go." Not surprisingly, the therapy didn't go well. The randomly selected therapist seemed overwhelmed. Her husband had revenge sex with one of his coworkers. "Ultimately we couldn't work through it," says Louise. One day she just announced that she didn't think the marriage could be fixed. "I think I felt too guilty, like 'I'm a bad person and I have to take myself away from you.'" The two separated, and both later married new partners. Their daughter travels between the two countries.

Ada's experience with therapy was a little different. She

discovered her husband of eighteen years was cheating on her in 2003. She kicked him out and within a few months was seeing other guys. "I was totally over the marriage and thought it had a zero chance of survival," she says. But her husband kept importuning her to give him another shot. After the split, she had started seeing a therapist, who eventually suggested trying some sessions that included him. "It took a long, long, long, long time to reestablish trust, but we found our way back together and we made a much stronger and better couple," says Ada, who credits her therapist. "Never could have done it without her; I am a stubborn and unforgiving type." The two had a second wedding, even though they'd never divorced, and their therapist was a guest. They recently celebrated their thirty-second wedding anniversary.

Betraying your spouse is a horrible, crappy, selfish, and stupid thing to do. If you get caught, you will break your lover's heart. If you have children, you will break their hearts. Even if you don't get caught, you're robbing that person and your family of your time and probably your money, and you are destroying your chances for mutual intimacy by sharing your heart with another person and by lying again and again to your partner. And then lying some more to cover up those lies. Almost as hard to stomach, several cheaters told me, is the fact that you are not living up to your own ideals of who you are. You are betraying your own values, unless you're the kind of person who grew up hoping to consistently deceive someone who loves you. Of course, affairs always seem more fun than marriages: there are no onerous domestic commitments, there are vats full of novelty, and there's no difficult history. And, even more delicious, they're forbidden. But they usually prove to be brief emotional insurgencies rather than revolutionary new love stories. Most affairs, according to pioneering infidelity specialist Shirley Glass (mother of *This American Life*'s Ira Glass), do not turn into marriages. In her experience only 10 percent of people who left their relationships for affairs ended up with the affair partner.

On the other hand, infidelity does not always have to spell the end of an otherwise loving partnership. And that's where a counselor can help. Take Wendi and Keith. Wendi couldn't believe it when she found strange texts on her husband's iPad. They had raised three kids together, seen each other through the death of family members, supported each other's careers. But there was no denying it; Keith, straightest of the straight arrows, was way too intimate with a colleague. Wendi had started seeing a therapist and was telling him about it, puzzling over why her husband was talking to his colleagues in a way he didn't talk to her, when the therapist put words to what she couldn't say. "He's having an affair," he said. "We just don't know what type yet."

For his part, Keith had had a traumatic stretch. Several disasters had befallen friends and family in quick succession and he was the rock, stepping in when others needed him, organizing, advocating, being a shoulder to cry on. He wasn't spending much time at home, and when he did, it seemed to him that his wife was more litigator than lover. He fell into an affair with one of the coworkers he was counseling. But after a few years, he began having serious misgivings. This wasn't who he thought he was. He and his wife were committed Christians and he couldn't understand how he had betrayed everything he believed in.

So when Wendi came to him and said gently that she knew he had developed a relationship with another woman, that she had been seeing a therapist privately and that she thought he should come, too, his immediate reaction, he says, was relief. They saw a counselor twice a week for six months. Slowly he admitted the extent of the relationship. Slowly he came to understand that after an affair there is no friendship; that person is now a no-go zone. It was not a gentle exit; his affair partner was outraged. But Wendi and Keith recommitted to each other. They figured out how to change the way they were reacting to each other so that their love was more clearly expressed. They read books and drew on the considerable resources on the Internet on recovering from infidelity. Wendi began to heal.

"I want people to know that you can come back from this," says Keith. "That your marriage can be stronger

than ever. Going through this improved our relationship."
(Of course, there are less painful ways to get the same result.)

Karl Pillemer, the researcher who delved deeply into
the marriages of seven hundred elderly couples, says he
was taken aback by how many of them had strayed once
but had worked through it. "In a surprising number of
cases, a single case of infidelity was not considered to be
an automatic end as long as there was reconciliation, remorse, and often counseling," he says. Mind you, there
was a limit. Serial cheating led to almost certain division
of the marital assets.

GETTING OVER THE WORST

The most conservative estimates suggest that more than
25 percent of married men and about 15 percent of married women have sex with somebody who is not their
spouse over the course of their relationships. That percentage, almost certainly an underestimate, is quite high,
especially considering that unlike divorce, adultery is still
pretty much universally frowned upon and the numbers
aren't budging much in the face of the technological revolution and Ashley Madison. Three-quarters of Americans
believed that it is always wrong to have sex with "someone

other than your spouse" in 2016, which is roughly the same proportion that felt that way in 1991. A further 13 percent believed that cheating is *almost* always wrong, just as they did twenty-five years ago.[8] This attitude is not merely true of puritanical Americans. A 2002[9] study that surveyed attitudes regarding cheating around the world found that no matter "a culture's notion of descent [whether lineage passes through the father or the mother], level of social complexity, or the degree to which a culture is normatively permissive or restrictive in sexual matters," everybody wants spouses to keep it in the home. (The exception here may be gay men, for whom sexual fidelity appears to be less important than emotional loyalty, but the research on this mostly predates the arrival of legal gay marriage.)

Recently there has been a rise in interest in open marriages and in polyamory among heterosexual couples, in which people form a small nest of lovers. Fundamentalist Mormons and others have scored some legal victories for their version of togetherness. But these are still outliers. Therapists warn that open marriages are much harder to maintain than they look. Even if couples can deal with the jealousy, the interpersonal mathematics is convoluted. The interaction between just two partners is already prone to complications and misunderstanding; throw in another one and the complexity goes off the charts. After counseling several polyamorous couples, therapist and author Daphne de Marneffe concluded that the sheer amount of communication and scheduling involved would exhaust most people.[10] (She also advised people who wanted to try opening up their marriages to wait until there were no more kids at home.)

How do you come back from a betrayal of the order of magnitude of infidelity? Very slowly. Depending on the type of liaison—full-blown affair or a little too much Facebook intimacy—therapists suggest that it takes about two years for a person who has been betrayed to feel completely safe around a spouse again. The betraying spouse has to of course agree to cut off all contact with the affair partner, but that's just the start of it. It's not just the lying down with someone else, say therapists, it's the lying to your partner that causes the corrosion. So it requires transparency and openness of a whole different order of magnitude, including sometimes, for a while, really Big Brothery stuff such as complete access to phones and computers and a lot of reassurance about whereabouts. If you've cheated on your spouse, your spouse's natural assumption is that you no longer love him or her, and you are untrustworthy. You have to go out of your way to prove otherwise.

People who have been cheated on feel violated and betrayed, but they also report having all the confidence forced out of them with one swift kick. What is wrong with them that their lover had to look elsewhere? Why is their love not enough? Are they too fat, ugly, weak, boring, unsuccessful? Studies have shown that the trauma of discovery can affect the way they parent and work and trigger depression. As impossible as this may sound, however, therapists say they should try not to take a partner's betrayal personally. Often cheaters are not unhappy with their spouses at all; they're unhappy with their lives and their relationships. They're trying to solve their problems in a way that they decline to see as damaging. Keith still loved his wife; he was unhappy with the way they were together.

Ada says one of the reasons she and her spouse reunited was that she had major foot surgery and could barely get around. Her husband was her rock during that time, taking her to appointments and making sure she had what she needed. But he remained very respectful in their former home. He didn't try to move back in. "He was very committed to it succeeding," she says. She didn't ask for access to his phone or email but he often offered information. Basically, he had to persuade her of his love all over again.

There are several schools of thought as to why people have affairs. Attachment theory offers one explanation: cheaters cheat because they learned from childhood that those closest to them were unreliable, and therefore they need a backup plan when they begin to feel dependent on a person. Social constructionist theory focuses on cultural socialization (everyone does it; it's natural), and investment models posit that cheaters aren't getting the satisfaction, investment, and commitment from the relationship that they desire, so they seek it elsewhere. Other studies suggest it's a combination of outside factors, personality types, and issues within the marriage. New York divorce lawyer James J. Sexton puts it more succinctly in his book on how not to get divorced. "If We Were Designing an Infidelity-Generating Machine," one of his chapters is called "It Would Be Facebook." The combination of yearning for youth, the ability to make life look idyllic online, and the ease of secret communication has been great for his business. Whatever the reason, it's pretty hard to come back from a marital-trust annihilation attempt of that order without getting professional help. Therapy doesn't work for everyone, but few people can get through the trauma without it. (Louise's affair partner eventually reunited with his wife without the aid of therapy, but said he wouldn't recommend doing it that way.) And, as the old political saying goes: Never let a good crisis go to waste.

YOU COULD ALWAYS SERVICE IT

Fixing a marriage is hard and exhausting. What might be a smarter approach, especially for younger couples, is getting some preventative help before things go too far off the road. Current figures suggest that the highest percentage of marriages that don't work out come to grief within the first ten years.[11] (More than 20 percent of marriages don't make it that far.) There are lots of reasons for this ("Hello, youth? It's impulsivity calling!"), but one that is often overlooked is that we have built a culture of marriage that is heavily front-loaded. The wedding is seen as the end-point, the culmination. People want to get married so much, and the wedding takes up so much of the heat and light, that it obscures the inconvenient reality that after the wedding they will be living with each other forever. We expend a squillion times more effort thinking about our weddings than we do about the marriage that will come after, which is like buying into a high-stakes poker game and then figuring out how to play.

There's always a bumpy period early in a marriage where the crazy, stupid, wonderful, romantic infatuation begins to wilt, like a flower, and transform into the more hardy and useful companionate love, like fruit. This is also the time when patterns of interaction begin to emerge—how a couple communicates, how two people resolve conflicts, how they make space for each other's dreams and challenges. One longitudinal study[12] showed that partners' personalities change during the first eighteen months of marriage and not necessarily in helpful ways: both become less agreeable, for example. This is when all the attitudes and habits that we imbibed from our family of origin begin to emerge, shaken into the open like mice whose nests are disturbed during construction.

It's easy for young people to think that if they go to counseling at that point, they're lame. "The good things that came out of marriage therapy would have come out of individual therapy," says Max, who went to therapy with his wife after two years of being married. "I got the sneaking suspicion that our therapist was keeping track of which spouse was ganged up on and alternated from session to session." He's still married but he's not sure the therapy helped. "In hindsight, the arrangement didn't give either one of us space to find our own voices so we both felt unfairly represented on a fairly regular basis."

A more useful alternative for young couples might be relationship education. This is different from therapy in that couples are not asked to reveal personal information, the work is done in a group, and there are exercises to practice with each other rather than one therapist guiding a couple through. And a key point: it's cheaper. My husband and I have done two and they're still pretty damn awkward, but as with learning anything, it's liberating to at least try a different way of doing something.

For one of them, we had to do a sort of mind-reading exercise, where we told our spouses what we thought they thought about a certain subject, by finishing the sentence "I'm wondering if you think . . ." For example, "I'm wondering if you think I am not doing a good job with the kids," or "I'm wondering if you think we watch too much TV," or, of course, "I'm wondering if you think we should eat less butter?" Our spouses then had an opportunity to clarify their views or perspective on a subject. While it's a very kabuki and stylized way to communicate, the exercise did demonstrate the role that expectations and the misunderstanding of such can play in a relationship.

There are some studies[13] that suggest that this type of relationship training actually improves people's couple communication skills and happiness—even among the trickiest of newlyweds, those who moved in together more from happenstance than by choice. And while it feels unnatural to practice this stuff, that doesn't make it bad. Lots of pursuits that are good are not natural, including mechanical engineering, making margaritas, and monogamy. "The foundation of relationship practice is the insight that just as people don't have problems, they *are* problems," writes Terrence Real, "good relationship is not something you have but something you *do*."[14]

WHEN DIVORCING JUST LOOKS EASIER

Should all couples be encouraged to stay together, especially if they're young and don't have kids, or a lot of
shared property, yet? Or is the better course to simply dust
yourselves off and walk away and try again? It's a hard
call. Therapists claim they can help most couples, no matter how distressed. But they also agree that nobody should
stay in a relationship if they are in physical danger, or any
member of their family is. For couples where one of the
partners has a mental illness or an addiction, the future
looks grim. Many therapists say little can be done if people can't be weaned off their "misery stabilizers:" drugs,
alcohol, gambling, extramarital sex. And there are definitely people who got married for the wrong reasons—
they needed to get away from their parents or they thought
nobody else would ask them or one of them was preg-
nant. It cannot be stressed enough that prevention in these
cases is so much better than cure.

In 2000, about half of the citizens of the United States
believed that a divorce should be more difficult to get than
it was at the time. But that figure has since dropped, and
as of 2016, only 38 percent of the country would like the
divorce laws to be stricter, which is the exact same proportion as would like them to be looser.[15] The United States is

as pro-divorce as it has been since the folks at the University of Chicago started polling people about their attitudes in 1972. No-fault divorce is now the law of the land, as well as in most Western democracies. This is a good and healthy thing—splitting up is a miserable enough journey without a legal minefield to wade through—but it also means people sometimes move on before their time.

Divorcing sometimes just looks easier than fixing a marriage, in the same way that buying new headphones often looks easier than untangling the ones you have. I have a friend who periodically drops by my place to complain about his marriage (another perk of being a writer about family life). Actually mostly what he does is complain about his wife, whom, because he is a scientist, he calls "emotionally disequilibrated." I always end up giving him the same advice about divorce. It means half as much access to his kids, half as much access to his money, and more or less the same amount of access to his wife. Nobody should stay married for the "sake of the kids" if a marriage has become untenable or, worse, abusive. But nobody should have any blinders on when it comes to the reality of divorce.

The study[16] that checked in with 645 unhappy couples after five years found that those who had gone on to divorce were no happier than those who had not. And those who stayed together were glad that they hadn't divorced, even though the problems they had five years ago were not resolved. In another study,[17] 34 percent of married Oklahomans reported that, at some point in the past, they thought their marriage was in serious trouble and considered divorce. Of those, 92 percent reported that they were glad they were still together. Even those mid-divorce are sometimes not too sure about it. A 2016 study[18] of parents who had filed for divorce but had not yet finalized it found that a quarter of them were ambivalent about splitting and 8 percent of them were fully opposed. (One casualty of no-fault divorce laws is people who don't want to get divorced; if their spouses say they're done, they're done.)

People's satisfaction with their marriages, it has long been suggested by psychologists, is like their satisfaction with their lives, U-shaped. I prefer to think of it like a riverbed. It starts off pretty high with the promise of independence and a life spent with a best friend. Then, as kids and responsibilities and disappointments and the cranks of age arrive, marriage increasingly begins to feel like slow going, with lots of slippery obstacles and slimy leg brushes coming at you. Satisfaction begins to dip. It stays low for a while and then ever so slowly begins to get better. Eventually the deep waters subside and the joyful part of marriage reemerges. You just have to forge on and keep your head above water.

That 2002 study of unhappy marriages found that often, things didn't get better, they just get easier to tolerate. "Many spouses said that their marriages got happier, not because they and their partner resolved problems but because they stubbornly outlasted them,"[19] the authors wrote. One of the secrets of staying married is simply declining to divorce, even when it seems like an enticing option. This doesn't mean grinning and bearing it—although a little of that is occasionally called for—but not giving up. We have a solving mentality, some therapists say, when in fact, what we often need is a carousel mentality; sometimes your horse is down, but if you wait a while, it will rise again.

If you have any doubts about divorce, then therapy is something that might be worth trying first. There are many types, nearly all with annoying acronyms like PREP or PAIRS or IBCT. So if you tried one—perhaps one that really focused on your family history—with only tepid results, you might try another. Some therapists are more experiential than others—that is, they want the two of you to have an interaction in front of them and to intervene and show you a different way of reacting. Therapy can be expensive, so after you've consulted friends, your local faith-based institutions, and/or the Internet for recommendations, call a few and see how they respond to your concerns. This is particularly helpful if a partner actually has a psychiatric condition or is self-medicating. If you have a specific problem—money, parenting, or sex—that seems insoluble, you might try to find someone who spe-

cializes in that. Many do not charge for the first consulta-
tion. Also, it should be stated that marital therapy is not
usually as expensive as lawyers, the therapy your kids
might need later, or even dividing your family's assets.

Almost a decade after we finished couples counseling,
from a time when I peeked over into the chasm of what life
might be like without him, I love my husband more than
ever. By that I mean I feel more affection for him and his
blue eyes and his voice and how he always walks a bit like
he's on a ship and his wild, unkempt hair and the way that
his stubble outlines his chin dimple and his very slow wandering way of constructing a sentence out loud, but also
that I am constantly quietly seeking ways to make his life
better, fine-tuning the way I behave around him to be more
caring. This sounds exhausting, but it actually feels more
absorbing. It's like what I imagine it must feel like to make
small adjustments in order to play an instrument better or
improve your golf swing. Learning your spouse is fun and
vaguely satisfying, like getting better at cryptic cross-
words. And I feel loved by him. I mean, not enough but
close.

My spouse, as I think I mentioned, is a long-term guy.
He makes/buys/attempts things that take a long time to
come to fruition and last a long time. The way architects
do. I'm more your novelty queen, learning new stuff
quickly, then moving quickly to the next idea, the next

story, the bright shiny thing a little farther up the beach. So, for me, marriage is that rare thing, a skill I have worked on to reach more than adequacy. This is the longest I've ever stuck at any project and I'm not done yet. I'm so grateful for it.

I do not mean that I never do anything selfish or stupid or careless or that I never hurt him or choose myself above him. That's probably still the majority of the time. I do not mean that he does not sometimes make me completely unhinged with frustration. Nor do I mean that we are both superior people, who now deserve a good marriage. I mean that marriage—or long-term committed monogamy—has been good for us. Treating the joint venture that is us as something to treasure has worked its way into our personalities and ways of thinking and activities and has made our lives richer and brought us more joy than any other part of our lives. For me, anyway. He always has architecture.

ACKNOWLEDGMENTS

———

A large number of people have been ridiculously generous in helping me to write this book. People have handed over information they learned over many hard years of therapy and study. People have told me their most intimate stories, many of which were painful to recount. My family members have consented to have personal tales told about them and not been too hard on me when our memories differed. But most contributors who wish to be acknowledged have been named. So I just want to mention the others.

The research on this book was aided immeasurably by my association with *Time* magazine, my beloved employer, which I really believe makes me and all its readers smarter every week. The folks there taught me so much about how to take an interesting subject and turn it into a story, how to research and write and check that what you wrote is true and how to be fair and accurate while still being fun to read. And they've not only put up with this random loud Australian in their story meetings and newsroom but have taken her in as one of their own, even if she can't pronounce the word *chart*. I've worked for six managing editors and I'm grateful to them all, but I'd be remiss not to mention my friend and mentor Richard Stengel; Nancy Gibbs, who first set me on the path of writing about marriage; and her successor, Edward Felsenthal, who has encouraged me to continue to try to write research-based stories on subjects that are often dismissed as too soft.

This book began as a cover story edited by the indefatigable Susanna Schrobsdorff. My colleague Jeff Kluger then pretty much scolded me into transforming it to something bigger. My agent and friend Betsy Lerner, who sought me out twenty years ago and took me to lunch for years before I ever looked like a prospective author, patiently took me through the process of book-writing without ever once calling me a numbskull. Julie Grau, my editor at Spiegel and Grau, who really cared about the subject, made the whole process so much less scary than I thought it would be. Carey Wallace was a friend and confidante and early reader and a post to tie myself to when the hurricanes of self-doubt blew through. Susan Weill painstakingly fact-checked for me.

On a more personal note, I'm indebted to Sue Pincusoff, for guiding my husband and me through a tough period in our marriage and helping us see what a partnership could be. I need to thank my parents, not only for staying married but for being such a source of great material. And thanks to my kids, who must be so sick of hearing "I can't, I have to finish my book" by now. And most of all, I have to thank Jeremy, the most difficult and worthwhile husband in the world. Thanks for letting me tell our stories. Thanks for goading me into a more interesting life. And thanks for marrying me.

Three Dozen Questions
for Intimacy

In a 1997 experiment, psychologists Arthur and Elaine Aron and their team tried to ascertain if it is possible to generate closeness. They got students to perform a variety of tasks and then measured how much more intimate they had become. One of their most successful tools was a suite of thirty-six questions, divided into three sets, with each set requiring more self-disclosure than the last. These were later published by *The New York Times* and framed as a way of falling in love with someone else, but they're useful for spouses and their friends as well. The original study was published in the academic journal *Personality and Social Psychology Bulletin*,[1] and Dr. Aron has allowed us to republish them here. He recommends taking no more than fifteen minutes to answer each section and then staring into your partner's eyes for four minutes.

SET I

1. Given the choice of anyone in the world, whom would you want as a dinner guest?

2. Would you like to be famous? In what way?

3. Before making a telephone call, do you ever rehearse what you are going to say? Why?

4. What would constitute a "perfect" day for you?

5. When did you last sing to yourself? To someone else?

6. If you were able to live to the age of ninety and retain either the mind or body of a thirty-year-old for the last sixty years of your life, which would you want?

7. Do you have a secret hunch about how you will die?

8. Name three things you and your partner appear to have in common.

9. For what in your life do you feel most grateful?

10. If you could change anything about the way you were raised, what would it be?

11. Take four minutes and tell your partner your life story in as much detail as possible.

12. If you could wake up tomorrow having gained any one quality or ability, what would it be?

SET II

13. If a crystal ball could tell you the truth about yourself, your life, the future or anything else, what would you want to know?

14. Is there something that you've dreamed of doing for a long time? Why haven't you done it?

15. What is the greatest accomplishment of your life?

16. What do you value most in a friendship?

17. What is your most treasured memory?

18. What is your most terrible memory?

19. If you knew that in one year you would die suddenly, would you change anything about the way you are now living? Why?

20. What does friendship mean to you?

21. What roles do love and affection play in your life?

22. Alternate sharing something you consider a positive

characteristic of your partner. Share a total of five items.

23. How close and warm is your family? Do you feel your childhood was happier than most other people's?

24. How do you feel about your relationship with your mother?

SET III

25. Make three true "we" statements each. For instance, "We are both in this room, feeling . . ."

26. Complete this sentence: "I wish I had someone with whom I could share . . ."

27. If you were going to become a close friend with your partner, please share what would be important for him or her to know.

28. Tell your partner what you like about them; be very honest this time, saying things that you might not say to someone you've just met.

29. Share with your partner an embarrassing moment in your life.

30. When did you last cry in front of another person? By yourself?

31. Tell your partner something that you like about them already.

32. What, if anything, is too serious to be joked about?

33. If you were to die this evening with no opportunity to communicate with anyone, what would you most regret not having told someone? Why haven't you told them yet?

34. Your house, containing everything you own, catches fire. After saving your loved ones and pets, you have time to safely make a final dash to save any one item. What would it be? Why?

35. Of all the people in your family, whose death would you find most disturbing? Why?

36. Share a personal problem and ask your partner's advice on how he or she might handle it. Also, ask your partner to reflect back to you how you seem to be feeling about the problem you have chosen.

NOTES

CHAPTER 1

1. Terrence Real, *The New Rules of Marriage: What You Need to Know to Make Love Work* (New York: Ballantine Books, 2008), 8.
2. Eli J. Finkel, *The All or Nothing Marriage: How the Best Marriages Work* (New York: Dutton, 2017), 83.
3. J. Yamada, M. Kito, and M. Yuki, "Passion, Relational Mobility, and Proof of Commitment: A Comparative Socio-Ecological Analysis of an Adaptive Emotion in a Sexual Market," *Evolutionary Psychology* (October–December 2017): 1–8, https://doi.org/10.1177/1474704917746056.
4. Finkel, *The All or Nothing Marriage*, 24.
5. L. Campbell and S. Moroz, "Humour Use Between Spouses and Positive and Negative Interpersonal Behaviours During Conflict," *Europe's Journal of Psychology* 10, no. 3 (2014): 532–42, https://doi.org/10.5964/ejop.v10i3.763.

6. Ibid., ironically.

7. Elizabeth A. Robinson and M. Gail Price, "Pleasurable Behavior in Marital Interaction: An Observational Study," *Journal of Consulting and Clinical Psychology* 48, no. 1 (1980): 117–18, https://doi.org/10.1037/0022-006X.48.1.117.

8. R. L. Weiss, "Strategic behavioral marital therapy: Toward a model for assessment and intervention, Volume 1." In J. P. Vincent, ed., *Advances in family intervention, assessment and theory* (Greenwich, CT: JAI Press, 1980), 229–71.

9. T. J. Loving, E. E. Crockett, and A. A. Paxson, "Passionate Love and Relationship Thinkers: Experimental Evidence for Acute Cortisol Elevations in Women," *Psychoneuroendocrinology* 34, no. 6 (2009): 939–46, https://doi.org/10.1016/j.psyneuen.2009.01.010.

10. A. W. Barton, T. G. Futris, and R. B. Nielsen, "Linking Financial Distress to Marital Quality: The Intermediary Roles of Demand/Withdraw and Spousal Gratitude Expressions," *Personal Relationships* 22, no. 3 (2015): 536–49, https://doi.org/10.1111/pere.12094.

11. N. M. Lambert and F. D. Fincham, "Expressing Gratitude to a Partner Leads to More Relationship Maintenance Behavior," *Emotion* 11, no. 1 (2011): 52–60, https://doi.org/10.1037/a0021557.

12. Jon Jecker and David Landy, "Liking a Person as a Function of Doing Him a Favor," *Human Relations* 22, no. 4 (1969): 371–78, https://doi.org/10.1177/001872676902200407.

13. J. Dew and W. Bradford Wilcox, "Generosity and the Maintenance of Marital Quality," *Journal of Marriage and Family* 75, no. 5 (2013): 1218–28, https://doi.org/10.1111/jomf.12066.

14. J. R. Olson, J. P. Marshall, H. W. Goddard, and D. G. Schramm, "Shared Religious Beliefs, Prayer, and Forgiveness as Predictors of Marital Satisfaction," *Family Relations* 64, no. 4 (2015): 519–33, https://doi.org/10.1111/fare.12129.

15. F. D. Fincham and S. R. Beach, "I say a little prayer for you: Praying for partner increases commitment in romantic relationships," *Journal of Family Psychology,* no. 28 (2014): 587–93, https://doi.org/10.1037/a0034999.

16. S. R. Beach, T. R. Hurt, F. D. Fincham, K. J. Franklin, L. M. McNair, and S. M. Stanley, "Enhancing Marital Enrichment through Spirituality: Efficacy Data for Prayer Focused Relationship Enhancement," *Psychology of Religion and Spirituality* 3, no. 3 (2011): 201–16, https://doi.org/10.1037/a0022207.

17. Charlotte Reissman, Arthur Aron, and Merlynn R. Bergen, "Shared Activities and Marital Satisfaction: Causal Direction and Self-Expansion versus Boredom," *Journal of Social and Personal Relationships* 10, no. 2 (1993): 243–54, https://doi.org/10.1177/026540759301000205.

18. William Ruger, Sven E. Wilson, and Shawn L. Waddoups, "Warfare and Welfare: Military Service, Combat, and Marital Dissolution," *Armed Forces and Society* 29, no. 1 (2002): 85–107, https://doi.org/10.1177/0095327X0202900105.

19. James K. McNulty, Michael A. Olson, Rachael E. Jones, and Laura M. Acosta, "Automatic Associations between One's Partner and One's Affect as the Proximal Mechanism of Change in Relationship Satisfaction: Evidence from Evaluative Conditioning," *Psychological Science* 28, no. 8 (2017): 1031–40, https://doi.org/10.1177/0956797617702014.

20. Irene Tsapelas, Arthur Aron, and Terri Orbuch, "Marital Boredom Now Predicts Less Satisfaction 9 Years Later," *Psychological Science* 20, no. 5 (2009): 543–45, https://doi.org/10.1111/j.1467-9280.2009.02332.x.

21. Irum Abbasi and Nawal Alghamdi, "The Pursuit of Romantic Alternatives Online: Social Media Friends as Potential Alternatives," *Journal of Sex and Marital Therapy* 44, no. 1 (2018): 16–28, https://doi.org/10.1080/00926 23X.2017.1308450.

22. For a full list of the questions, please see Appendix.

23. D. W. Crawford, R. M. Houts, T. L. Huston, and L. J. George, "Compatibility, Leisure, and Satisfaction in Marital Relationships," *Journal of Marriage and Family* 64, no. 2 (2004): 433–49, https://doi.org/10.1111/j.1741-3737.2002.00433.x.

24. Real, *The New Rules of Marriage,* 13.

25. D. J. Knapp, J. A. Durtschi, C. E. Clifford, J. G. Kimmes, P. Barros-Gomes, and J. Sandberg, "Self-esteem and Caregiving in Romantic Relationships: Self- and Partner Perceptions," *Personal Relationships* 23, no. 1 (2016): 111–23, https://doi.org/10.1111/pere.12114.

26. G. E. Birnbaum and H. T. Reis, "When Does Responsiveness Pique Sexual Interest? Attachment and Sexual Desire in Initial Acquaintanceships," *Personality and Social Psychology Bulletin* 38, no. 7 (2012): 946–58, https://doi.org/10.1177/0146167212441028.

CHAPTER 2

1. Kira S. Birditt, Edna Brown, Terri L. Orbuch, and Jessica M. McIlvane, "Marital Conflict Behaviors and Implications for Divorce over 16 Years," *Journal of Marriage and Family* 72, no. 5 (2010): 1188–1204, https://doi.org/10.1111/j.1741-3737.2010.00758.x.

2. Stan Tatkin, "Relationships Are Hard, But Why?" TEDxKC, 2016. Retrieved from www.youtube.com/watch?v=2xKXLPuju8U.

3. Sun Tzu, *The Art of War* (Minneapolis Filiquarian Publishing, 2006: 7).

4. Tara R. McRae, Tracy L. Dalgleish, Susan M. Johnson, Melissa Burgess-Moser, and Kyle D. Killian, "Emotion Regulation and Key Change Events in Emotionally Focused Couple Therapy," *Journal of Couple and Relationship Therapy* 13, no. 1 (2014): 1–24, https://doi.org/10.1080/15332691.2013.836046.

5. Harriet Lerner, *Why Won't You Apologize?: Healing Big Betrayals and Everyday Hurts* (New York: Touchstone, 2017), 81.

6. Sun Tzu, *The Art of War,* 9.

7. Lerner, *Why Won't You Apologize?,* 47.

8. Real, *The New Rules of Marriage,* 52.

9. J. M. Gottman and R. W. Levenson, "A Two-Factor Model for Predicting When a Couple Will Divorce: Exploratory Analyses Using 14-Year Longitudinal Data," *Family Process* 41, no. 1 (2002): 83–96, https://doi.org/10.1111/j.1545-5300.2002.40102000083.x.

10. Real, *The New Rules of Marriage,* 83.

11. L. L. Carstensen, J. M. Gottman, and R. W. Levenson, "Emotional Behavior in Long-term Marriage," *Psychology and Aging* 10, no. 1 (1995): 140–49, www.ncbi.nlm.nih .gov/pubmed/7779311; R. W. Levenson, L. L. Carstensen, and J. M. Gottman, "Influence of Age and Gender on Affect, Physiology, and Their Interrelations: A Study of Long-term Marriages," *Journal of Personality and Social Psychology* 67, no. 1 (1994): 56–68, www.ncbi.nlm.nih.gov /pubmed/8046584.

12. J. M. Gottman, *What Predicts Divorce?: The Relationship between Marital Processes and Marital Outcomes* (Hillsdale, NJ: Lawrence Erlbaum, 1994); J. M. Gottman, J. Coan, S. Carrere, and C. Swanson, "Predicting Marital Happiness and Stability from Newlywed Interactions," *Journal of Marriage and the Family* 60, no. 1 (1998): 5–22, https://doi.org/10.2307/353438.

13. Birditt, Brown, Orbuch, and McIlvane, "Marital Conflict Behaviors and Implications for Divorce over 16 Years."

14. T. Bradbury, S. Campbell, and F. Fincham, "Longitudinal and Behavioral Analysis of Masculinity and Femininity in Marriage," *Journal of Personality and Social Psychology* 68, no. 2 (1995): 328–41, https://www.ncbi.nlm.nih.gov /pubmed/7877096.

15. H. M. Maranges and J. K. McNulty, "The Rested Relationship: Sleep Benefits Marital Evaluations," *Journal of Family Psychology* 31, no. 1 (2017): 117–22, https://doi .org/10.1037/fam0000225.

16. P. R. Amato and A. Booth, "The Legacy of Parents' Marital Discord: Consequences for Children's Marital Quality," *Journal of Personality and Social Psychology* 81, no. 4

(2001): 627–38, http://dx.doi.org/10.1037/0022–3514.81.4
.627.

17. Michael McCullough, Lindsey Root Luna, Jack Berry, Benjamin Tabak, and Giacomo Bono, "On the Form and Function of Forgiving: Modeling the Time-Forgiveness Relationship and Testing the Valuable Relationships Hypothesis," *Emotion* 10, no. 3 (2010): 358–76, https://doi
.org/10.1037/a0019349.

18. Lerner, *Why Won't You Apologize?*, 52.

19. Miles Hewstone, Ed Cairns, Alberto Voci, Juergen Hamberger, and Ulrike Niens, "Intergroup Contact, Forgiveness, and Experience of 'The Troubles' in Northern Ireland," *Journal of Social Issues* 62, no. 1 (2006): 99–120, http://dx.doi.org/10.1111/j.1540-4560.2006.00441.x.

20. Janis Abrahms Spring with Michael Spring, *How Can I Forgive You? The Courage to Forgive, the Freedom Not To* (New York: Perennial Currents, 2005), 124.

21. Michael McCullough, Eric J. Pedersen, Evan Carter, and Benjamin A. Tabak, "Conciliatory Gestures Promote Human Forgiveness and Reduce Anger," *Proceedings of the National Academy of Sciences* 111, no. 30 (2014): 11211–16, https://doi.org/10.1073/pnas.1405072111.

22. Michael McCullough, *Beyond Revenge: The Evolution of the Forgiveness Instinct* (San Francisco: Jossey-Bass, 2008); Filippo Aureli and Frans B. M. de Waal, *Natural Conflict Resolution* (Berkeley, CA: University of California Press, 2000).

23. D. J. Hruschka and J. Henrich, "Friendship, cliquishness, and the emergence of cooperation," *Journal of Theoretical Biology* 239 (2006): 1–15.

24. 1 Corinthians 13:5.

25. McCullough, Root Luna, Berry, et al, "On the Form and Function of Forgiving," *Emotion* 10, no. 3 (2010): 358–76, https://doi.org/10.1037/a0019349.

26. Ibid.

27. M. E. McCullough, L. M. Root, and A. D. Cohen, "Writing about the Personal Benefits of a Transgression Facilitates Forgiveness," *Journal of Consulting and Clinical Psychology* 74, (2006): 887–97, https://doi .org/10.1037/0022-006X.74.5.887.

CHAPTER 3

1. Scott I. Rick, Deborah A. Small, and Eli J. Finkel, "Fatal (Fiscal) Attraction: Spendthrifts and Tightwads in Marriage," *Journal of Marketing Research* 48, no. 2 (2011): 228–37, https://doi.org/10.1509/jmkr.48.2.228.

2. S. M. Stanley, H. J. Markman, and S. W. Whitton, "Communication, Conflict, and Commitment: Insights on the Foundations of Relationship Success from a National Survey," *Family Process* 41, no. 4 (2002): 659–75, https://doi .org/10.1111/j.1545-5300.2002.00659.x.

3. J. P. Dew and J. Dakin, "Financial Disagreements and Marital Conflict Tactics," *Journal of Financial Therapy* 2, no. 1 (2011): 22–42, https://doi.org/10.4148/jft.v2i1.1414.

4. L. M. Papp, E. M. Cummings, and M. C. Goeke-Morey, "For Richer, for Poorer: Money as a Topic of Marital Conflict in the Home," *Family Relations* 58, no. 1 (2009): 91–103, https://doi.org/10.1111/j.1741-3729.2008.00537.x.

5. Ibid.

6. Pamela J. Smock, Wendy D. Manning, and Meredith Por-
    ter, " 'Everything's There Except Money': How Money
    Shapes Decisions to Marry among Cohabitors," *Journal
    of Marriage and Family* 67, no. 3 (2005): 680–96, https://
    doi.org/10.1111/j.1741-3737.2005.00162.x.

7. K. M. Shuey and A. E. Wilson, "Economic Hardship in
    Childhood and Adult Health Trajectories: An Alternative
    Approach to Investigating Life-course Processes," *Ad-
    vances in Life Course Research* 22 (2014): 49–61, http://doi
    .org/10.1016/j.alcr.2014.05.001.

8. Experian Credit and Divorce Survey, https://www.experian
    .com/blogs/ask-experian/survey-results-when-divorce-does
    -damage-to-your-credit/.

9. K. D. Vohs, N. L. Mead, and M. R. Goode, "The Psycho-
    logical Consequences of Money," *Science* 314, no. 5802
    (2006): 1154–56, https://doi.org/10.1126/science.1132491.

10. L. R. Dean, J. S. Carroll, and C. Yang, "Materialism, Per-
    ceived Financial Problems, and Marital Satisfaction," *Fam-
    ily and Consumer Sciences Research Journal* 35, no. 3
    (2007): 260–81, https://doi.org/10.1177/1077727X06296625.

11. N. P. Li, A. J. Y. Lim, M.-H. Tsai, and J. O, "Too Material-
    istic to Get Married and Have Children?," *PLoS ONE* 10,
    no. 5 (2015): e0126543, https://doi.org/10.1371/journal
    .pone.0126543.

12. Ibid.

13. D. G. Myers, *Exploring Social Psychology*, 4th ed. (New
    York: Worth, 2007).

14. S. L. Britt, E. J. Hill, A. B. LeBaron, D. R. Lawson, and
    R. A. Bean, "Tightwads and Spenders: Predicting Financial
    Conflict in Couple Relationships," *Journal of Financial*

Planning 30, no. 5 (2017): 36–42, www.onefpa.org/journal
/Pages/MAY17-Tightwads-and-Spenders-Predicting
-Financial-Conflict-in-Couple-Relationships.aspx.

15. Scott Hankins and Mark Hoekstra, "Lucky in Life, Un-
lucky in Love?: The Effect of Random Income Shocks on
Marriage and Divorce," *Journal of Human Resources* 46,
no. 2 (2011): 403–26, https://doi.org/10.3368/jhr.46.2.403.

16. N. Shenhav, "What Women Want: Family Formation and
Labor Market Responses to Marriage Incentives," (Job
Market Paper, University of California, Davis, January 12,
2016), https://economics.ucr.edu/seminars_colloquia/2015
-16/applied_economics/Shenhav%20paper%20for%20
2%204%2016%20job%20talk%20seminar.pdf.

17. R. Fry and D. Cohn, *New Economics of Marriage: The
Rise of Wives,* Pew Research Center, 2010, www.pewtrusts
.org/en/research-and-analysis/reports/2010/01/19/new
-economics-of-marriage-the-rise-of-wives.

18. Christin L Munsch, "Her Support, His Support: Money,
Masculinity, and Marital Infidelity," *American Sociological
Review,* Vol. 80, Issue 3 (2015): 469–495, https://doi
.org/10.1177/0003122415579989

19. L. Pierce, M. S. Dahl, and J. Nielsen, "In Sickness and in
Wealth: Psychological and Sexual Costs of Income Comparison in Marriage," *Personality and Social Psychology
Bulletin* 39, no. 3 (2013): 359–74, https://doi.org/10.1177
/0146167212475321.

20. Marta Murray-Close and Misty L. Heggeness, "Manning
up and womaning down: How husbands and wives report
their earnings when she earns more," June 06, 2018, Working Paper Number: SEHSD-WP2018-20, https://www

.census.gov/content/dam/Census/library/working-papers
/2018/demo/SEHSD-WP2018-20.pdf.

21. Vladas Griskevicius, Joshua M. Tybur, Jill M. Sundie,
Robert B. Cialdini, Geoffrey F. Miller, and Douglas T.
Kenrick, "Blatant Benevolence and Conspicuous Consumption: When Romantic Motives Elicit Strategic Costly Sig-
nals," *Journal of Personality and Social Psychology* 93, no. 1
(2007): 85–102, http://dx.doi.org/10.1037/0022-3514.93.1.85.

22. R. T. Pinkus, P. Lockwood, U. Schimmack, and M. A.
Fournier, "For Better and for Worse: Everyday Social Comparisons Between Romantic Partners," *Journal of Personality and Social Psychology* 95, no. 5 (2008): 1180–1201,
https://doi.org/10.1037/0022-3514.95.5.1180.

23. Andrew E. Clark and Andrew J. Oswald, "Satisfaction and
Comparison Income, *Journal of Public Economics* 61,
no. 3 (1996): 359–81, https://doi.org/10.1016/0047
-2727(95)01564-7; Erzo F. P. Luttmer, "Neighbors as Nega-
tives: Relative Earnings and Well-Being," *Quarterly Journal of Economics,* Vol. 120 (Aug. 2005, Issue 3): 963–1002,
http://users.nber.org/~luttmer/relative.pdf.

24. Olle Folke and Johanna Rickne, "All the Single Ladies: Job
Promotions and the Durability of Marriage," Working
Paper Number 1146, Research Institute of Industrial Eco-
nomics, Stockholm, 2016.

25. Christine R. Schwartz and Pilar Gonalons-Pons, "Trends
in Relative Earnings and Marital Dissolution: Are Wives
Who Outearn Their Husbands Still More Likely to Divorce?," *Russell Sage Foundation Journal of the Social Sciences* 2, no. 4 (2016): 218–36, www.rsfjournal.org/doi
/full/10.7758/RSF.2016.2.4.08.

26. Pinkus, "For Better and for Worse: Everyday Social Comparisons Between Romantic Partners."

27. M. Shapiro, "Money: A Therapeutic Tool for Couples Therapy," *Family Process* 46, no. 3 (2007): 279–91, https://doi.org/10.1111/j.1545-5300.2007.00211.x.

28. Joanna Pepin, "Normative Beliefs about Money in Families: Balancing Togetherness, Autonomy, and Equality," *SocArXiv*, updated July 2, 2018, https://doi.org/10.17605/OSF.IO/6AQSE.

29. "Survey Results: When Divorce Does Damage to Your Credit," Experian.com, January 2017. This was an online survey of five hundred adults who had been divorced in the last five years.

30. Erin El Issa, "2016 American Household Credit Card Debt Study," NerdWallet.com, www.nerdwallet.com/blog/credit-card-data/household-credit-card-debt-study-2016/.

31. J. P. Dew, "Debt Change and Marital Satisfaction Change in Recently Married Couples," *Family Relations* 57, no. 1 (2008): 60–71, https://doi.org/10.1111/j.1741-3729.2007.00483.x.

32. J. P. Dew and J. Dakin, "Financial disagreements and marital conflict tactics," *Journal of Financial Therapy,* Vol. 2, Issue 1, Article 7 (2011), https://doi.org/10.4148/jft.v2i1.1414.

33. K. Archuleta, E. Rasure, J. Boyle, and E. Burr, "Do Couples Need to Be on the Same Page?: Exploring Shared Financial Goals as a Mediator for Financial Anxiety, Financial Satisfaction, and Relationship Satisfaction," *Consumer Interests Annual* 59 (2013): 1–3, https://www.consumerinterests.org/assets/docs/CIA/CIA2013

/Posters2013/archuleta%20rasure%20boyle%20burr%20
-%20do%20couples%20need%20to.pdf.

34. S. A. Burt, M. B. Donnellan, M. N. Humbad, B. M. Hicks,
M. McGue, and W. G. Iacono, "Does Marriage Inhibit An-
tisocial Behavior?: An Examination of Selection vs. Causation via a Longitudinal Twin Design," *Archives of General
Psychiatry* 67, no. 12 (2010): 1309–15, https://doi
.org/10.1001/archgenpsychiatry.2010.159.

35. Megan de Linde Leonard and T. D. Stanley, "Married with
children: What remains when observable biases are re-
moved from the reported male marriage wage premium,"
Labour Economics Vol. 33 (Apr. 2015): 72–80. https://
EconPapers.repec.org/RePEc:eee:labeco:v:33:y:2015:i
:c:p:72-80.

36. Jay L. Zagorsky, "Marriage and Divorce's Impact on
Wealth," *Journal of Sociology* 41, no. 4 (2005): 406–24,
https://doi.org/10.1177/1440783305058478.

37. Janet Wilmoth and Gregor Koso, "Does Marital History
Matter?: Marital Status and Wealth Outcomes among
Preretirement Adults," *Journal of Marriage and the Family* 64, no. 1 (2004): 254–68, https://doi.org/10.1111
/j.1741-3737.2002.00254.x.

38. Volker Ludwig and Josef Brüderl, "Is There a Male Marital Wage Premium? New Evidence from the United States,"
American Sociological Review, 83, no. 4, (2018) 744–770
https://doi.org/10.1177/0003122418784909.

39. Barbara A. Butrica and Karen E. Smith, "The Retirement
Prospects of Divorced Women," *Social Security Bulletin*
72, no. 1 (2012): 11–22, www.ssa.gov/policy/docs/ssb
/v72n1/v72n1p11.html.

CHAPTER 4

1. J. Belsky and M. Rovine, "Patterns of Marital Change across the Transition to Parenthood: Pregnancy to Three Years Postpartum," *Journal of Marriage and Family* 52, no. 1 (1990): 5–19, https://doi.org/10.2307/352833; C. P. Cowan and P. A. Cowan, *When Partners Become Parents: The Big Life Change for Couples* (Mahwah, NJ: Lawrence Erlbaum, 1992).

2. M. J. Cox, B. Paley, M. Burchinal, and C. C. Payne, "Marital perceptions and interactions across the transition to parenthood," *Journal of Marriage and the Family* 61 no. 3 (1999): 611–25, http://dx.doi.org/10.2307/353564.

3. A. F. Shapiro, J. M. Gottman, and S. Carrère, "The Baby and the Marriage: Identifying Factors That Buffer against Decline in Marital Satisfaction after the First Baby Arrives," *Journal of Family Psychology* 14, no. 1 (2000): 59–70, https://doi.org/10.1037//0893-3200.14.1.59; E. S. Kluwer, J. A. Heesink, and E. Vliert, "The Division of Labor across the Transition to Parenthood: A Justice Perspective," *Journal of Marriage and Family* 64, no. 4 (2002): 930–43, https://doi.org/10.1111/j.1741-3737.2002.00930.x; Julie M. Koivunen, Jeanne W. Rothaupt, and Susan M. Folfgram, "Gender Dynamics and Role Adjustment during the Transition to Parenthood: Current Perspectives," *Family Journal* 17, no. 4 (2009): 323–28, https://doi.org/10.1177/1066480709347360.

4. Kim Parker and Wendy Wang, "Modern Parenthood: Roles of Moms and Dads Converge as They Balance Work and

Family," Pew Research Center, Social and Demographic
Trends, March 14, 2013, www.pewsocialtrends
.org/2013/03/14/modern-parenthood-roles-of-moms-and
-dads-converge-as-they-balance-work-and-family/.

5. Bureau of Labor Statistics, American Time Use Survey,
    "Charts by Topic: Household Activities," 2016, www.bls
    .gov/tus/charts/household.htm.

6. Bureau of Labor Statistics, Economic News Release,
    "Table 5. Employment Status of the Population by Sex,
    Marital Status, and Presence and Age of Own Children
    under 18, 2016–2017 Annual Averages," 2016, www.bls
    .gov/news.release/famee.t05.htm.

7. Parker and Wang, "Modern Parenthood, Roles of Moms
    and Dads Converge as They Balance Work and Family."

8. T. Hansen, "Parenthood and Happiness: A Review of Folk
    Theories versus Empirical Evidence," *Social Indicators Research* 108, no. 1 (2012): 29–64, https://doi.org/10.1007
    /s11205-011-9865-y.

9. J. M. Twenge, W. K. Campbell, and C. A. Foster, "Parenthood and Marital Satisfaction: A Meta-analytic Review,"
    Journal of Marriage and Family 65, no. 3 (2003): 574–83,
    https://doi.org/10.1111/j,1741-3737.2003.00574.x; K. M.
    Nomaguchi and M. A. Milkie, "Costs and Rewards of
    Children: The Effects of Becoming a Parent on Adults'
    Lives," *Journal of Marriage and Family* 65, no. 2 (2003):
    356–74, https://doi.org/10.1111/j.1741-3737.2003.00356.x.

10. S. Offer, "Time with Children and Employed Parents'
    Emotional Well-being," *Social Science Research* 47
    (2014):192–203, https://doi.org/10.1016/j.ssresearch
    .2014.05.003.

11. Josh Coleman quoted in Sharon Meers and Joanna Strober, *Getting to 50/50: How Working Couples Can Have It All by Sharing It All: And Why It's Great for Your Marriage, Your Career, Your Kids, and You* (New York: Bantam Books, 2009), 189.

12. L. E. Kotila, S. J. Schoppe-Sullivan, and C. M. Kamp Dush, "Time in Parenting Activities in Dual-Earner Families at the Transition to Parenthood," *Family Relations* 62, no. 5 (2013): 795–807, PMCID: PMC4578481, www.ncbi.nlm.nih.gov/pubmed/26405367.

13. Parker and Wang, "Modern Parenthood, Roles of Moms and Dads Converge as They Balance Work and Family."

14. M. Lino, K. Kuczynski, N. Rodriguez, and T. Schap, *Expenditures on Children by Families, 2015,* Miscellaneous Publication No. 1528–2015, U.S. Department of Agriculture, Center for Nutrition Policy and Promotion, 2017, www.cnpp.usda.gov/sites/default/files/crc2015.pdf.

15. R. G. Lucas-Thompson, W. A. Goldberg, and J. Prause, "Maternal Work Early in the Lives of Children and Its Distal Associations with Achievement and Behavior Problems: A Meta-analysis," *Psychological Bulletin* 136, no. 6 (2010): 915–42, https://doi.org/10.1037/a0020875; *The NICHD Study of Early Child Care and Youth Development: Findings for Children up to 4½ Years,* U.S. Department of Health and Human Services, National Institutes of Health, National Institute of Child Health and Human Development, 2006, www1.nichd.nih.gov/publications/pubs/documents/seccyd_06.pdf.

16. Ashley V. Whillans, Elizabeth W. Dunn, Paul Smeets, Rene Bekkers, Michael I. Norton, "Buying time promotes happiness," *Proceedings of the National Academy of Sciences*

Aug. 2017, 114 (32) 8523-8527; DOI: 10.1073/pnas
.1706541114.

17. M. O'Brien and K. Wall, eds., *Comparative Perspectives on
Work-Life Balance and Gender Equality—Fathers on Leave
Alone* (New York: Springer Open, 2017).

18. Society for Human Resource Management, "2018 Employee Benefits Survey—The Evolution of Benefits," Table
6, p. 25 (2018), https://www.shrm.org/hr-today/trends-and
-forecasting/research-and-surveys/Documents/2018%20
Employee%20Benefits%20Report.pdf.

19. N. K. Grote, M. S. Clark, and A. Moore, "Perceptions of
Injustice in Family Work: The Role of Psychological Distress," *Journal of Family Psychology* 18, no. 3 (2004):
480–92, https://doi.org/10.1037/0893-3200.18.3.480; Kotila,
Schoppe-Sullivan, Kamp Dush, "Time in Parenting Activities in Dual-Earner Families at the Transition to Parenthood"; A. R. Poortman and T. Van der Lippe, "Attitudes
toward Housework and Child Care and the Gendered
Division of Labor," *Journal of Marriage and Family*
71, no. 3 (2009): 526–41, https://doi.org/10.1111
/j.1741-3737.2009.00617.x.

20. William H. Jeynes, "Meta-analysis on the Roles of Fathers
in Parenting: Are They Unique?," *Marriage and Family Review* 52, no. 7 (2016): 665–88, https://doi.org/10.1080/0149
4929.2016.1157121.

21. C. S. Mott Children's Hospital, National Poll on Children's Health, *Mott Poll Report: Mom Shaming or Constructive Criticism? Perspectives of Mothers* 29, no. 3, June
19, 2017, https://mottnpch.org/reports-surveys/mom
-shaming-or-constructive-criticism-perspectives-mothers.

22. Jennifer Lehr, *Parentspeak: What's Wrong with How We*

Talk to Our Children—and What to Say Instead (New York: Workman, 2016).

23. S. Gable, J. Belsky, and K. Crinic, "Marriage, Parenting, and Child Development: Progress and Prospects," *Journal of Family Psychology* 5, nos. 3–4 (1992): 276–94, http://dx .doi.org/10.1037/0893-3200.5.3-4.276.

24. Timothy Keller and Kathy Keller, *The Meaning of Marriage: Facing the Complexities of Commitment with the Wisdom of God* (New York: Dutton, 2011), 142.

25. Ayelet Waldman, "Truly, Madly, Guiltily," *The New York Times,* March 27, 2005, www.nytimes.com/2005/03/27 /fashion/truly-madly-guiltily.html.

26. Chrystyna D. Kouros, Lauren M. Papp, Marcie C. Goeke-Morey, and E. Mark Cummings, "Spillover between Marital Quality and Parent–Child Relationship Quality: Parental Depressive Symptoms as Moderators," *Journal of Family Psychology* 28, no. 3 (2014): 315–25, http://dx.doi .org/10.1037/a0036804.

27. G. T. Harold, J. J. Aitken, and K. H. Shelton, "Interparental Conflict and Children's Academic Attainment: A Longitudinal Analysis," *Journal of Child Psychology and Psychiatry* 48, no. 12 (2007): 1223–32, https://doi .org/10.1111/j.1469-7610.2007.01793.x.

28. Stephanie L. McFall and Chris Garrington, eds., *Understanding Society: Early Findings from the First Wave of the UK's Household Longitudinal Study* (Colchester: Institute for Social and Economic Research, University of Essex, 2011), 11, http://repository.essex.ac.uk/9115/1 /Understanding-Society-Early-Findings.pdf.

29. Paul R. Amato, "The Consequences of Divorce for Adults

and Children," *Journal of Marriage and Family* 62 (2000): 1269–1287, https://doi:10.1111/j.1741-3737.2000.01269.x.

30. Lynn White, "The Effect of Parental Divorce and Remarriage on Parental Support for Adult Children," *Journal of Family Issues* 13, no. 2 (1992): 234–250, https://doi .org/10.1177/019251392013002007.

31. Judith Wallerstein, Julia Lewis, and Sandra Blakeslee, The Unexpected Legacy of Divorce: A 25-Year Landmark Study (New York: Hyperion, 2001), 298.

32. Paul R. Amato, Jennifer B. Kane, and Spencer James, "Reconsidering the 'Good Divorce,'" *Family Relations* 60, no. 5 (2011): 511–24, https://doi.org/10.1111 /j.1741-3729.2011.00666.x.

33. Shelly Lundberg, Robert A. Pollak, and Jenna Stearns, "Family Inequality: Diverging Patterns in Marriage, Cohabitation, and Childbearing," *The Journal of Economic Perspectives : A Journal of the American Economic Association* 30, no. 2, (2016): 79–102. http://doi.org/10.1257 /jep.30.2.79

34. S. A. Ruiz and M. Silverstein, "Relationships with Grandparents and the Emotional Well-being of Late Adolescent and Young Adult Grandchildren," *Journal of Social Issues* 63, no. 4 (2007): 793–808, https://doi.org/10.1111 /j.1540-4560.2007.00537.x.

35. R. Dunifon and A. Bajracharya, "The Role of Grandparents in the Lives of Youth," *Journal of Family Issues* 33, no. 9 (2012): 1168–94, https://doi.org/10.1177/0192513X12444271.

CHAPTER 5

1. *One-in-Five U.S. Adults Were Raised in Interfaith Homes,*
   Pew Research Center, October 26, 2016, www.pewforum
   .org/2016/10/26/one-in-five-u-s-adults-were-raised-in
   -interfaith-homes/; S. Elliott and D. Umberson, "The Performance of Desire: Gender and Sexual Negotiation in
   Long-Term Marriages," *Journal of Marriage and Family* 70, no. 2 (2008): 391–406, https://doi.org/10.1111
   /j.1741-3737.2008.00489.x.

2. Robert T. Michael, John H. Gagnon, Edward O. Laumann,
   and Gina Kolata, *Sex in America: A Definitive Survey*
   (Boston: Little, Brown, 1994).

3. Seth Stephens-Davidowitz, "Searching for Sex," *The New
   York Times,* January 24, 2015, www.nytimes.com/2015
   /01/25/opinion/sunday/seth-stephens-davidowitz
   -searching-for-sex.html.

4. J. M. Twenge, R. A. Sherman, and B. E. Wells, "Declines
   in Sexual Frequency among American Adults, 1989–2014,"
   Archives of Sexual Behavior 46, no. 8 (2017): 2389–2401,
   https://doi.org/10.1007/s10508-017-0953-1.

5. General Social Survey figures provided by Tom Smith, director of the General Social Survey at NORC by request.

6. George Pelecanos, *Hell to Pay: A Novel* (Boston: Little,
   Brown, 2002).

7. Esther Perel, "The Secret to Desire in a Long-term Relationship," TED talk, 2013.

8. L. A. Jordan and R. C. Brooks, "The Lifetime Costs of Increased Male Reproductive Effort: Courtship, Copulation
   and the Coolidge Effect," *Journal of Evolutionary Biology*

23, no. 11 (2010): 2403–9, https://doi.org/10.1111 /j.1420-9101.2010.02104.x.

9. Caitlyn Yoshiko Kandil, "Body-image studies explore the source of much of our anxiety," *Los Angeles Times,* March 27, 2016, http://www.latimes.com/socal/weekend/news/tn -wknd-et-0327-body-image-studies-20160327-story.html.

10. S. Kornrich, J. Brines, and K. Leupp, "Egalitarianism, Housework, and Sexual Frequency in Marriage," *American Sociological Review* 78, no. 1 (2013): 26–50, https:// doi.org/10.1177/0003122412472340.

11. D. L. Carlson, A. J. Miller, S. Sassler, and S. Hanson, "The Gendered Division of Housework and Couples' Sexual Relationships: A Reexamination," *Journal of Marriage and Family* 78, no. 4 (2016): 975–95, https://doi.org/10.1111 /jomf.12313.

12. D. L. Carlson, A. J. Miller, and S. Sassler, "Stalled for Whom? Change in the Division of Particular Housework Tasks and Their Consequences for Middle- to Low-Income Couples," *Socius: Sociological Research for a Dynamic World* 4 (2018): 1–17, https://doi .org/10.1177/2378023118765867.

13. William J. Becker, Liuba Belkin, and Sarah Tuskey, "Killing me softly: Electronic communications monitoring and employee and spouse well-being," *Academy of Management Proceedings,* 2018; 2018 (1): 12574 DOI: 10.5465 /AMBPP.2018.121.

14. Adrienne Lucas and Nicholas Wilson, "Does Television Kill Your Sex Life? Microeconomic Evidence from 80 Countries," NBER Working Paper Number 24882, August 2018.

15. Juliana M. Kling, JoAnn E. Manson, Michelle J. Naugh-

ton, Mhamed Temkit, Shannon D. Sullivan, Emily W. Gower, Lauren Hale, Julie C. Weitlauf, Sara Nowakowski, and Carolyn J. Crandall, "Association of Sleep Disturbance and Sexual Function in Postmenopausal Women," *Menopause* 24, no. 6 (2017): 604–12, https://doi.org/10.1097/GME.0000000000000824.

16. D. A. Kalmbach, J. T. Arnedt, V. Pillai, and J. A. Ciesla, "The Impact of Sleep on Female Sexual Response and Behavior: A Pilot Study," *The Journal of Sexual Medicine* 12, no. 5 (2015): 1221–32, https://doi.org/10.1111/jsm.12858.

17. Sarah Arpin, Cynthia Mohr, Alicia Starkey, Sarah Haverly and Leslie Hammer, "A Well Spent Day Brings Happy Sleep: Findings from a Dyadic Study of Capitalization Support," presented at 2017 convention of the Society for Personality and Social Psychology.

18. Gurit E. Birnbaum, Harry T. Reis, Moran Mizrahi, Yaniv Kanat-Maymon, Omri Sass, and Chen Granovski-Milner, "Intimately Connected: The Importance of Partner Responsiveness for Experiencing Sexual Desire," *Journal of Personality and Social Psychology* 111, no. 4 (2016): 530–46, https://doi.org/10.1037/pspi0000069.

19. William H. Masters and Virginia E. Johnson, *Human Sexual Response* (Boston: Little, Brown, 1970), 219.

20. Mary Roach, *Bonk: The Curious Coupling of Science and Sex* (New York: W. W. Norton, 2008), 302.

21. J. A. Hess and T. A. Coffelt, "Verbal Communication about Sex in Marriage: Patterns of Language Use and Its Connection with Relational Outcomes," *The Journal of Sex Research* 49, no. 6 (2012): 603–12, https://doi.org/10.1080/00224499.2011.619282.

22. T. A. Coffelt and J. A. Hess, "Sexual Disclosures: Connec-

tions to Relational Satisfaction and Closeness," *Journal of Sex and Marital Therapy* 40, no. 6 (2014): 577–91, https://doi.org/10.1080/0092623X.2013.811449.

23. S. Sprecher and R. M. Cate, "Sexual Satisfaction and Sexual Expression as Predictors of Relationship Satisfaction and Stability," in J. H. Harvey, A. Wenzel, and S. Sprecher, eds., *The Handbook of Sexuality in Close Relationships* (Mahwah, NJ: Lawrence Erlbaum, 2004), 235–56; S. MacNeil and E. S. Byers, "Dyadic Assessment of Sexual Self-disclosure and Sexual Satisfaction in Heterosexual Dating Couples," *Journal of Personal and Social Relationships* 22, no. 2 (2005): 169–81, https://doi.org/10.1177/0265407505050942.

24. M. K. Pitts, A. M. Smith, J. Grierson, M. O'Brien, and S. Misson, "Who Pays for Sex and Why? An Analysis of Social and Motivational Factors Associated with Male Clients of Sex Workers," *Archives of Sexual Behavior* 33, no. 4 (2004): 353–58, https://doi.org/10.1023/B:ASEB.0000028888.48796.4f.

25. S. Sprecher, S. Metts, B. Burleson, E. Hatfield, and A. Thompson, "Domains of Expressive Interaction in Intimate Relationships: Associations with Satisfaction and Commitment," *Family Relations* 44, no. 2 (1995): 203–10, https://doi.org/10.2307/584810.

26. Pamela Regan and Leah Atkins, "Sex Differences and Similarities in Frequency and Intensity of Sexual Desire," *Social Behavior and Personality: An International Journal* 34, no. 1 (2006): 95–102, https://doi.org/10.2224/sbp.2006.34.1.95.

27. Jennifer M. Ostovich and John Sabini, "How Are Sociosexuality, Sex Drive, and Lifetime Number of Sexual Partners Related?," *Personality and Social Psychology*

Bulletin 30, no. 10 (2004): 1255–66, https://doi
.org/10.1177/0146167204264754.

28. P. Blumstein and P. Schwartz, *American Couples: Money,
Work, Sex* (New York: William Morrow, 1983).

29. B. Komisaruk, B. Whipple, A. Crawford, W. C. Liu,
A. Kalnin, and K. Mosier, "Brain Activation during
Vaginocervical Self-stimulation and Orgasm in Women
with Complete Spinal Cord Injury: fMRI Evidence of Me-
diation by the Vagus Nerves," *Brain Research* 1024,
nos. 1–2 (2004): 77–88, https://doi.org/10.1016
/j.brainres.2004.07.029.

30. D. Herbenick, M. Mullinax, and K. Mark, "Sexual Desire
Discrepancy as a Feature, Not a Bug, of Long-term Relationships: Women's Self-reported Strategies for Modulat-
ing Sexual Desire," *The Journal of Sexual Medicine* 11,
no. 9 (2014): 2196–206, https://doi.org/10.1111/jsm.12625.

31. Cathi Hanauer, ed., *The Bitch Is Back: Older, Wiser, and
(Getting) Happier* (New York: HarperCollins, 2016), 115.

32. Rosemary Basson, "The Female Sexual Response: A Different Model," *Journal of Sex and Marital Therapy* 26, no. 1
(2000): 51–65, https://doi.org/10.1080/009262300278641.

33. Rosemary Basson, "Rethinking low sexual desire in
women," *BJOG: An International Journal of Obstetrics &
Gynaecology* 109 (2002): 357–63, https://doi.org/10.1111
/j.1471-0528.2002.01002.x.

34. C. M. Meston and D. M. Buss, "Why Humans Have Sex,"
Archives of Sexual Behavior 36 (2007): 477–507, https://
doi.org/10.1007/s10508-007-9175-2.

35. Sari M. van Anders, Lisa Dawn Hamilton, Nicole Schmidt,
and Neil V. Watson, "Associations between Testosterone

Secretion and Sexual Activity in Women," *Hormones and Behavior* 51, no. 4 (2007): 477–82, https://doi.org/10.1016/j.yhbeh.2007.01.003.

36. Ibid.

37. Ellen McCarthy, "Psychologist Barry McCarthy Helps Couples Resolve Sex Problems," *The Washington Post*, December 6, 2009.

38. Michael Metz and Barry McCarthy, *Enduring Desire: Your Guide to Lifelong Intimacy* (New York: Routledge, 2011).

39. Amy Muise, Ulrich Schimmack, and Emily A. Impett, "Sexual Frequency Predicts Greater Well-being, But More Is Not Always Better," *Social Psychological and Personality Science* 7, no. 4 (2016): 295–302, https://doi.org/10.1177/1948550615616462.

40. S. Hite, *The Hite Report: A Nationwide Study of Female Sexuality* (New York: Dell, 1976).

41. K. S. Fugl-Meyer, K. Oberg, P. O. Lundberg, B. Lewin, and A. Fugl-Meyer, "On Orgasm, Sexual Techniques, and Erotic Perceptions in 18- to 74-Year-Old Swedish Women," *The Journal of Sexual Medicine* 3, no. 1 (2006): 56–68, https://doi.org/10.1111/j.1743-6109.2005.00170.x.

42. Barry R. Komisaruk and Beverly Whipple, "Functional MRI of the Brain during Orgasm in Women," *Annual Review of Sex Research* 16 (2005): 62–86, https://www.tandfonline.com/doi/abs/10.1080/10532528.2005.10559829.

43. Ibid.

44. J. R. Georgiadis, R. Kortekaas, R. Kuipers, A. Nieuwenburg, J. Pruim, A. A. Reinders, and G. Holstege, "Regional Cerebral Blood Flow Changes Associated with Clitorally

Induced Orgasm in Healthy Women," *European Journal of Neuroscience* 24, no. 11 (2006): 3305–16, https://doi.org/10.1111/j.1460–9568.2006.05206.x.

45. M. Chivers, M. Seto, and R. Blanchard, "Gender and Sexual Orientation Differences in Sexual Response to Sexual Activities Versus Gender of Actors in Sexual Films," *Journal of Personality and Social Psychology,* Vol. 93, No. 6 (2007): 1108–1121, https://doi.org/10.1037/0022-3514.93.6.1108.

46. Rachel Hills, *The Sex Myth: The Gap Between Our Fantasies and Reality* (New York: Simon & Schuster Paperbacks, 2015), 8.

47. T. Kohut, W. A. Fisher, and L. Campbell, "Perceived Effects of Pornography on the Couple Relationship: Initial Findings of Open-Ended, Participant-Informed, 'Bottom-Up' Research," *Archives of Sexual Behavior* 46, no. 2 (2017): 585–602, https://doi.org/10.1007/s10508-016-0783-6.

48. B. Y. Park, G. Wilson, J. Berger, M. Christman, B. Reina, F. Bishop, W. P. Klam, and A. P. Doan, "Is Internet Pornography Causing Sexual Dysfunctions? A Review with Clinical Reports," *Behavioral Sciences* 6, no. 3 (2016): 17, https://doi.org/10.3390/bs6030017.

49. E. L. Deci and R. M. Ryan, "The 'What' and 'Why' of Goal Pursuits: Human Needs and the Self-determination of Behavior," *Psychological Inquiry* 11, no. 4 (2000): 227–68, https://doi.org/10.1207/S15327965PLI1104_01.

50. B. McCarthy, "Sexual Desire and Satisfaction: The Balance between Individual and Couple Factors," *Sexual and Relationship Therapy* 27, no. 4 (2012): 310–21, https://doi.org/10.1080/14681994.2012.738904.

51. B. R. Komisaruk, C. Beyer-Flores, and B. Whipple, *The Science of Orgasm* (Baltimore: Johns Hopkins University Press, 2006).

52. G. Davey Smith, S. Frankel, and J. Yarnell, "Sex and Death: Are They Related? Findings from the Caerphilly Cohort Study," *The BMJ* 315, no. 7123 (1997): 1641–44, https://doi.org/10.1136/bmj.315.7123.1641.

53. Roach, *Bonk*, 39.

54. Karl Pillemer, *30 Lessons for Loving: Advice from the Wisest Americans on Love, Relationships and Marriage* (New York: Avery, 2015), p.181.

CHAPTER 6

1. One study did note parallels between Chapman's methods and other theoretical models: Nichole Egbert and Denise Polk, "Speaking the Language of Relational Maintenance: A Validity Test of Chapman's (1992) Five Love Languages," *Communication Research Reports* 23, no. 1 (2006): 19–26, https://doi.org/10.1080/17464090500535822.

2. Quoted in Susan Gilbert, "Married with Problems? Therapy May Not Help," *The New York Times,* April 19, 2005, www.nytimes.com/2005/04/19/health/psychology/married-with-problems-therapy-may-not-help.html.

3. M. Robin Dion, Sarah A. Avellar, Heather H. Zaveri, Debra A. Strong, Alan M. Hershey, Timothy J. Silman and Betsy Santos, "The Oklahoma Marriage Initiative: A Process Evaluation" May 23, 2008, research.policyarchive.org/15743.pdf.

4. According to National Directory of Marriage and Family Counseling, "Family and Marriage Counseling Cost: How Much Will It Cost?," www.counsel-search.com/articles/marriage-family-counseling_71.htm.

5. Douglas Wendt and Kevin Shafer, "Gender and Attitudes about Mental Health Help Seeking: Results from National Data," *Health & Social Work* 41, no. 1 (2016): e20–e28, https://doi.org/10.1093/hsw/hlv089.

6. L. J. Waite, D. Browning, W. J. Doherty, M. Gallagher, Y. Lou, and S. M. Stanley, *Does Divorce Make People Happy? Findings from a Study of Unhappy Marriages* (New York: Institute for American Values, 2002).

7. Rebecca Aponte, "Augustus Napier on Experiential Family Therapy," Psychotherapy.net, https://www.psychotherapy.net/interview/augustus-napier.

8. Tom W. Smith, Michael Davern, Jeremy Freese, and Michael Hout, General Social Surveys, 1972–2016, https://gssdataexplorer.norc.org/trends/Gender%20&%20Marriage?measure=xmarsex.

9. William Jankowiak, M. Diane Nell, and Anne Buckmaster, "Managing Infidelity: A Cross-cultural Perspective," *Ethnology* 41, no. 1 (2002): 85–101, http://dx.doi.org/10.2307/4153022.

10. Daphne de Marneffe, *The Rough Patch: Marriage, Midlife, and the Art of Living Together* (New York: Scribner, 2018), 104–8.

11. Rose M. Kreider and Renee Ellis, "Number, Timing, and Duration of Marriages and Divorces: 2009," *Current Population Reports,* P70–125, U.S. Census Bureau, Washington, DC, 2011, figure 5.

12. Justin Lavner, Brandon Weiss, Joshua Miller, and Benjamin R. Karney, "Personality Change Among Newlyweds: Patterns, Predictors, and Associations With Marital Satisfaction Over Time," *Developmental Psychology* 54 (2017), http://dx.doi.org/10.1037/dev0000491.

13. J. M. Randles, "Partnering and Parenting in Poverty: A Qualitative Analysis of a Relationship Skills Program for Low-Income, Unmarried Families," *Journal of Policy Analysis and Management* 33, no. 2 (2014): 385–412, https://doi.org/10.1002/pam.21742; R. G. Carlson, S. M. Barden, A. P. Daire, and J. Greene, "Influence of Relationship Education on Relationship Satisfaction for Low-Income Couples," *Journal of Counseling and Development* 92, no. 4 (2014): 418–27, https://doi.org/10.1002/j.1556-6676.2014.00168.x.

14. Real, *The New Rules of Marriage*, 77.

15. Tom W. Smith, Michael Davern, Jeremy Freese, and Michael Hout, General Social Surveys, 1972–2016, https://gssdataexplorer.norc.org/trends/Gender%20&%20Marriage?measure=divlaw.

16. Waite, Browning, Doherty, et al., *Does Divorce Make People Happy?*

17. C. A. Johnson, S. M. Stanley, N. D. Glenn, P. A. Amato, S. L. Nock, H. J. Markman, and M. R. Dion, *Marriage in Oklahoma: 2001 Baseline Statewide Survey on Marriage and Divorce* (S02096 OKDHS) (Oklahoma City, OK: Oklahoma Department of Human Services, 2002).

18. William J. Doherty, Steven M. Harris, and Katharine Wickel Didericksen, "A Typology of Attitudes toward Proceeding with Divorce among Parents in the Divorce Pro-

cess," *Journal of Divorce and Remarriage* 57, no. 1 (2016): 1–11, https://doi.org/10.1080/10502556.2015.1092350.

19. Waite, Browning, Doherty, et al., *Does Divorce Make People Happy?*

APPENDIX

1. Arthur Aron, Edward Melinat, Elaine N. Aron, Robert Darrin Vallone, and Renee J. Bator, "The Experimental Generation of Interpersonal Closeness: A Procedure and Some Preliminary Findings," *Personality and Social Psychology Bulletin* (1997) 23, 363–377, https://doi.org/10.1177/0146167297234003.

ABOUT THE AUTHOR

BELINDA LUSCOMBE has worked at *Time* magazine for twenty years. She has written widely about relationships, marriage, culture, parenting, and the evolving role of women in the twenty-first century. She has also written for *Vogue, The New York Times, Sports Illustrated, Fortune, Arena,* and many international publications. Born in Sydney, Australia, she now lives in New York City, where she has been married to an architect for twenty-eight years, which is like thirty-five in human years.

Facebook.com/biggirlpants
@luscombeland

ABOUT THE TYPE

This book was set in Sabon, a typeface designed by the well-known German typographer Jan Tschichold (1902–74). Sabon's design is based upon the original letterforms of sixteenth-century French type designer Claude Garamond and was created specifically to be used for three sources: foundry type for hand composition, Linotype, and Monotype. Tschichold named his typeface for the famous Frankfurt typefounder Jacques Sabon (c. 1520–80).